WEST CUMBERLAND AT WAR

By
JEFF WILSON
B.Ed., T.Eng.

First Published in 1999
by
Jeffrey Wilson
Bellevue House
Distington
CA14 4PU.

All rights reserved. No part of this book may be reproduced, stored or introduced into a retrieval system, or transmitted in any form or by any means (electronic, mechanical, photocopying, recording or otherwise) without the permission of J S Wilson.

The right of Jeffrey Wilson to be identified as author of this work has been asserted by him in accordance with the Copyright, Designs and Patents Act 1988.

ISBN 0 9534645 0 4

British Library Cataloguing-in-Publication Data:
A catalogue record is available for this book from the British Library

Printed by Derwent Press Printers

Cover - photography - J Wilson.
Badges - CGS Curiosity Shop, Main Street, Cockermouth

*For Bethany Jane
my
Grand-daughter*

Acknowledgements

My Sincere thanks are due to the following:

Tom Armstrong, I H McDonald, Ralph Pickering, Victor O'Connor, The Late Tom Mitchell Q.M, Capt. V H P Roberts, Glynis Peacock M.Ed, Paul Pederson, Harry Roberts, The staff of the Records Office, Whitehaven, John Lace, Richard Coyles, Kath Sharpe, The Late Arthur Gabbitas (ex-Aux. Unit Signals), Neville Ramsden, Betty Hopkins (Sites and Monuments Officer, CCC), Jeffrey E Dorman, Topham Picturepoint, John Laing plc, The Licencing Officer, Photographic Archive, The Imperial War Museum.

A word of special thanks to Miss Carol Sarsfield Hall, for the use of her father's books, and the late Gilbert Rothery for his proof reading skills.

Also Mr TR Kirton, Editor of *The West Cumberland Times and Star*, and Hilary Scott, Editor of the *Whitehaven News* for allowing me to use their newspaper's photographs, from the 39-45 era.

***

In 1988 an appeal was made by the Defence of Britain project for volunteers. I agreed to record the twentieth century defence sites in West Cumbria. This research led me to many interesting stories from various sources, which just had to be shared. It does not tell personal stories; those books have been written. Rather, it tells of organisations and procedures adopted in a effort to win the war, when the enemy was at one time only eighteen miles from our shores.

The author acknowledges a grant from the Norman Nicholson Memorial Fund.

The book also may also be used as a teaching aid, it covers parts of the History National Curriculum (1995).

Specifically:

> *Key Stage 1. 'Changes in the way of life of their family or adults.'*
>
> *Key Stage 2. Britain since 1930, (Subsection on impact of WW2.)*
>
> *Key Stage 3. Twentieth-Century World & GCSE Syllabi.*

***

TIMETABLE of WWII

9th	February	1939	Home Office to Provide shelters for 'At risk' Homes
10th	February	1939	Pope Pius X1, Opponent of Nazism, Dies.
24th	**February**	**1939**	**Blackshirts address cinema crowds, on Hagg Hill Workington.**
15th	March	1939	German Troops cross the Czech frontier.
29th	March	1939	Britain doubles the size of its Territorial Army (TA).
7th	April	1939	Italy Invades Albania.
28th	April	1939	Hitler rips up the Polish non-aggression pact.
22nd	May	1939	Italian & German pact of steel.
29th	July	1939	British Government 'purges' IRA, after explosion.
23rd	August	1939	Germany & Russia sign non-aggression pact.
30th	August	1939	1.5 million British children evacuated to safe areas.
1st	September	1939	Dawn-Germany invades Poland.
1st	**September**	**1939**	**Egremont - 750 Evacuees (Children) arrive by Train.**
1st	**September**	**1939**	**First Evacuees arrive in Whitehaven, Workington, Egremont & Millom**
3rd	September	1939	Britain Issues Germany with a 9 am, ultimatum - WAR DECLARED
5th	September	1939	Workington Artillerymen leave for France.
6th	September	1939	Battle of Barking Creek. Start of the 'Phony' War.
6th	September	1939	Fighting on the French border, Identity cards introduced in Britain.
16th	September	1939	Petrol rationing begins in Britain.
28th	**September**	**1939**	**Distington welcomes 62 Evacuees from Newcastle.**
29th	September	1939	Poland surrenders.
1st	October	1939	British Men aged 20/22 eligible for Conscription.
11th	October	1939	British Expeditionary Force (BEF) in France numbers 158,000 men.
8th	November	1939	Assassination attempt on Hitler.
13th	November	1939	First Bombs fall on British Isles- Shetland
30th	November	1939	Soviet Union Invades Finland.
13th	December	1939	Battle of the River Plate.
19th	December	1939	First Canadian Troops arrive in Britain.
22nd	December	1939	Women Munitions workers demand equal pay with men.
1st	January	1940	Conscription, now for Men aged 20/27 years.
8th	January	1940	Rationing Begins in Britain.
15th	January	1940	Black-outs; twice as many people killed on roads.
17th	January	1940	Coldest Weather for 50 Years, Blizzards, River Thames Freezes.
18th	**January**	**1940**	**St. Bees School Foundation wing burns down.**
21st	**January**	**1940**	**Grand Hotel Whitehaven, destroyed by fire, 1 person Killed.**
29th	February	1940	Film, "Gone With the Wind", wins Academy awards.
13th	March	1940	Russia and Finland sign peace treaty, after conflict.
6th	April	1940	Germany attacks Greece & Yugoslavia.
8th	April	1940	Germany Invades Norway & Denmark.
8th	**April**	**1940**	**Ritz Cinema-special screening of 'The Stars Look Down.' Local scenes.**
10th	April	1940	Battle of Narvik.
1st	May	1940	Norway surrenders. British Troops Evacuated.
9th	May	1940	Conscription - upper age now 36.
10th	May	1940	First Bombs fall on England.
10th	May	1940	Germany attacks Belgium & Holland.
14th	**May**	**1940**	**Local Defence Volunteers Created - Thousands of Cumbrian's Enlist.**
15th	May	1940	Dutch surrender.
22nd	May	1940	Emergency Powers Act passed in Britain.
26th	May	1940	Operation Dynamo-Evacuation of British, French, and Belgian Troops Over 338,226 Allied Troops lifted of the beaches at Dunkirk.
30th	May	1940	Britain's signposts & street names removed as an Invasion precaution.
4th	June	1940	Germans seize Dunkirk.
10th	June	1940	Italy declares War on the Allies

13th June	1940	Britain's Church bells to be rung only as Invasion Signal.
14th June	1940	Germans enter Paris.
15th June	**1940**	**First Danish Fishing Boats arrive at Whitehaven.**
25th June	1940	Cease Fire in France.
28th June	1940	De Gaulle now leader of the 'Free French'.
29th June	1940	Germans occupy Guernsey
1st July	1940	Germans occupy Jersey.
10th July	1940	Start of the 'Battle of Britain'.
16th July	**1940**	**Air Raid on Silloth wounds 8 people.**
21st July	**1940**	**Air Raid on Maryport kills 7 and wounds 5 people.**
22nd July	**1940**	**First 'Alarm and Despondency' Prosecution at Whitehaven.**
7th August	**1940**	**Aeroplane - Handly Page 42E, crashes at West Croft farm Pica no injuries**
12th August	1940	Wasting Food now against the Law.
18th August	1940	Air Raids and Aerial Battles over Southern England.
24th August	1940	London Blitz begins.
1st September	1940	Britain exchanges leases on naval bases for 50 destroyers from USA.
3rd September	1940	Auxillary Fire Service (AFS) formed.
10th September	1940	Buckingham Palace Bombed amid weeks of London's blitz.
19th September	**1940**	**Incendiary Bombs fall on Barrow - No causalities.**
21st September	1940	Date for Hitler's Operation 'Sealion'-the Invasion of England. (postponed).
24th September	1940	The King introduces the George Cross and the George Medal.
30th September	1940	More Daylight Raids on Britain.
9th October	1940	Hitler's Invasion of Britain postponed; RAF Gains Air Superiority.
10th October	**1940**	**Distington ARP warden killed on duty.**
27th October	**1940**	**Air Raid on Workington - no causalities.**
5th November	1940	Franklin D. Roosevelt is elected as President of the USA for third time.
14th November	1940	Coventry bombed-554 civilians die.
15th November	1940	RAF bombs Hamburg.
30th November	1940	London, Birmingham, Southhampton, Sheffield, Manchester, Glasgow, Coventry, Dover, Liverpool, and Brighton have suffered bomb damage, in the last few months; over 4,588 killed and 6,200 wounded.
7th December	**1940**	**Whitehaven's air raid shelters opened.**
12th December	1940	British troops capture 30,000 Italians in Egypt.
30th December	1940	Request by British Miners for a bigger beef ration turned down.
2nd January	**1941**	**Air Raid on Millom kills 8 and wounds 11 people.**
8th January	1941	Lord Baden-Powell dies.
10th January	1941	Air attacks on Malta begin.
21st January	1941	British and Australian Troops capture Tobruk.
6th February	**1941**	**Whitehaven's Oldest pub 'T'Wooden Steps', burns down.**
7th February	**1941**	**Maryport adopts HMS Mangrove; £62,000 raised in Warship Week.**
10th February	1941	Iceland is bombed by Luftwaffe.
12th February	1941	First successful trial of Penicillin at Oxford.
3rd March	1941	German troops advance through Bulgaria towards Greece & Yugoslavia.
17th March	1941	Minister of Labour calls for women to staff factories & release men.
25th March	**1941**	**Vickers Wellington Bomber crashes at Frizington, no injuries.**
29th March	**1941**	**Whitehaven & Ennerdale RDC 'War Weapons Week'. £276,941 raised.**
6th April	1941	Germany invades Greece & Yugoslavia.
16th April	**1941**	**Landmine Explodes on the 'Big Green' Eskdale, - damage to property. Barrow Bombed - Abbey Rd, Ritz Cinema, Baths and Church damaged.**
17th April	1941	Yugoslavian Army surrenders.
19th April	**1941**	**Barrow Bombed again.**
21st April	1941	Greek Army surrenders.
6th May	**1941**	**Lockheed Hudson crashes at Loweswater - Pilot Killed.**
7th May	**1941**	**Barrow's Railway Station bombed.**
8th May	**1941**	**Vickers at Barrow bombed. Total of 70 Persons killed, in 4 Raids.**

10th May	1941	Large Air raid on London-1,436 killed.
10th May	1941	National Fire Service (NFS) formed.
13th May	1941	Rudolph Hess, Hitler's deputy parachutes into Scotland.
20th May	1941	German paratroopers land on Crete.
22nd May	**1941**	**10 Bombs land on Birker Moor - no injuries.**
27th May	1941	German Battleship 'The Bismarck' sunk.
1st June	1941	Britain Clothes rationing starts.
3rd June	**1941**	**William Pit explosion kills 12, injures 11.**
6th June	**1941**	**H.M.S. Whitehaven arrives on station at Alexandria**
		Whitehavens Spitfire 'Scawfell' enters service with 610 Squadron.
8th June	1941	Large Air raid by RAF on Germany, over 360 planes used.
22nd June	1941	Germany invades Russia.
4th July	1941	Coal rationing introduced in Britain.
7th July	**1941**	**Duke of Kent visits Maryport, Workington, and Whitehaven.**
10th July	**1941**	**ATC Squadron formed in Whitehaven.**
12th July	1941	Britain signs pact with Russia.
26th August	1941	Germany admits to losses of 440,000 men, on the Russian front.
27th August	1941	British Government commandeers Railways-pays compensation.
6th September	1941	All Jews in Germany forced to wear a yellow star of David.
15th September	1941	Siege of Leningrad.
18th October	**1941**	**Three Dutch Fascists in yacht stolen from IOM, run aground at Eskmeals**
19th October	1941	Siege of Moscow
7th November	1941	Churchill states: "Britain's resolve is unconquerable."
13th November	1941	German troops in Russia suffer as temperature falls to -22 .
7th December	1941	Japan declares war, and attacks Pearl Harbour.
8th December	1941	Canada declares war on Japan.
11th December	1941	Germany & Italy declare war on USA.
19th December	1941	Hong Kong falls to the Japanese.
28th December	**1941**	**Lockheed Hudson Bomber crashes at Dearham, 3 crew-members killed.**
1st January	1942	Pit tragedy in Stoke-on-Trent kills 57 miners.
21st January	1942	Australia asks for reinforcements.
26th January	1942	US Troops arrive in Northern Ireland.
14th February	**1942**	**Start of Whitehaven's 'Warship Week' appeal, HMS Whitehaven adopted.**
15th February	1942	Singapore falls to the Japanese.
19th February	1942	Japanese bomb Darwin Australia, killing 240 people.
21st February	**1942**	**Start of Workington's 'Warship Week' appeal. HMS Porpoise (sub) adopted**
21st March	1942	Britain has now spent more than the total budget of WW1.
27th March	**1942**	**Explosive device kills 2 Boys, on Workington's Northside shore.**
31st March	1942	Allied convoy arrives at Murmansk.
15th April	1942	Malta awarded the George Cross.
25th April	1942	Princess Elizabeth registers for War Service - aged 16.
5th May	1942	Battle of the Coral Sea begins.
11th May	1942	U Boat torpedoes US Merchant Ship, in the mouth of the Mississippi river.
31st May	1942	Cologne devastated by RAF, 2,000 tons of bombs dropped.
4th June	1942	Battle of Midway - Turning point in Pacific War.
22nd June	1942	Cairo under threat from Rommel.
23rd June	**1942**	**Sea Hurricane crashes at Dovenby - Pilot killed.**
26th June	**1942**	**Hawker Hurricane crashes at Black How, Cleator - Pilot killed.**
6th July	1942	British 8th Army forces Rommel to retreat.
10th July	1942	Convoy PQ 17 reaches Russia; 29 Ships lost.
31st July	1942	Oxfam formed.
3rd August	**1942**	**Start of Whitehaven & Ennerdale RDC. 'Tanks for Attack' appeals (£66,000)**
7th August	1942	US Marines land on Guadalcanal.
12th August	1942	General Montgomery takes over the 8th Army (Desert Rats).
24th August	1942	Duke of Kent killed in flying boat crash.

10th September	1942	RAF bombs Dusseldorf.
16th September	1942	German Army reaches Stalingrad.
11th October	1942	Joe Lewis quits boxing.
30th October	1942	Afrika Korps surrounded at El Alamein.
8th November	1942	Operation Torch - Landings at Algiers, Oran, and Casablanca.
15th November	1942	8th Army wins at El Alamein.
23rd November	1942	German 6th Army trapped at Stalingrad.
31st December	1942	Battle of the Barents Sea.
14th January	1943	Churchill, Roosevelt and De Gaulle attend Casablanca conference.
31st January	1943	Germans surrender at Stalingrad, their first Defeat.
2nd February	**1943**	**Sea Defence mines exploded by Army, damage to Crosscannonby.**
4th February	**1943**	**Sea Defence mines exploded by Army, damage to Flimby School & House.**
8th February	1943	Russians liberate Kursk.
14th February	1943	Chindits now across the River Chindwin.
18th February	1943	Row in the Commons over the date for introducing the 'Welfare State'.
2nd March	1943	RAF bombs Berlin.
11th March	**1943**	**Scotby, Carlisle, bombed 1 killed, 2 wounded.**
28th March	1943	Sergei Rachmaninov the Composer dies in Beverly Hills.
15th April	1943	Stuttgart bombed by RAF with 8,000lbs Blockbuster Bombs.
3rd May	1943	Part-time War work compulsory for British women between 18 and 45.
8th May	1943	Start of Whitehaven & Ennerdale RDC. 'Wings for Victory Week' -£365,331, raised.
14th May	**1943**	**Royal Ordnance Factory at Sellafield starts production of explosives.**
17th May	1943	617 Squadron of the RAF, carry out the Dambuster Raids.
31st May	**1943**	**Avro Anson & Wellington Bomber in mid air collision over Maryport; 6 Crew die.**
1st June	1943	Film actor Leslie Howard dies when his Airliner is shot down.
12th June	1943	Lady Baden-Powell, Chief Guide, visits Whitehaven and Seascale.
19th June	1943	Goebbels reports Berlin is 'Free of Jews'.
5th July	1943	Germany and Russia fight the war's largest tank battle at Kursk.
10th July	1943	Allied forces invade Sicily.
22nd July	1943	General Patton & US 7th Army seize Palermo, Sicily.
25th July	1943	Mussolini resigns.
27th July	1943	RAF bomb Hanover and cause a firestorm.
14th August	1943	Rome declared 'an open city.'
25th August	1943	Admiral Mountbatten now Supreme Allied Commander-South East Asia.
3rd September	1943	Invasion of Italy.
12th September	1943	Mussolini escapes from prison, helped by German Paratroops.
14th September	**1943**	**B17, Flying Fortress crashes at Keswick, 11 American Crewmen Die.**
22nd September	1943	PAYE introduced, tax now deducted at source.
13th October	1943	Italy declares War on Germany.
14th October	**1943**	**Avro Anson Bomber explodes over Arrowthwaite, Whitehaven - 5 crew killed.**
19th October	1943	4,220 Prisoners 'swapped.'
26th October	**1943**	**Hawker Hurricane crashes at Loughrigg, St Bees - Pilot killed.**
29th October	1943	London Dockers strike.
6th November	1943	Russian troops recapture Kiev.
2nd December	1943	German Battle-Cruiser, 'Scharnhörst' sunk.
6th December	1943	Ernest Bevin, Minister of Labour, creates 'Bevin Boys', (Young miners by ballot).
22nd December	1943	Beatrix Potter dies.
18th January	**1944**	**Explosion at RNAD, Broughton Moor - 11 people die, many injured**
19th January	1944	Russian Army moves into Poland.
22nd January	1944	Allies land at Anzio.
27th January	1944	Siege of Leningrad (900 days) ends.

2nd February	1944	French males between the ages of 16 and 20 forced to work in Germany.
15th February	1944	Monte Cassino Abbey destroyed.
18th February	1944	Another Blitz on London.
28th February	**1944**	**Wellington Bomber crashes into sea off Workington-1 crewman drowns.**
1st March	1944	Chindits enter Burma.
24th March	1944	Major-General Orde Wingate dies in plane crash.
28th March	1944	Men & women teachers to have equal pay.
2nd April	1944	Russian Troops invade Rumania.
20th April	1944	London Bus drivers on Strike.
27th April	1944	Invasion preparations, no visitors allowed within 10 miles of the coast.
30th April	1944	First Pre-fab houses on show in London.
2nd May	**1944**	**A Miles Martinet crashes at Seascale, 20 year old ATC Cadet wins BEM for rescue.**
3rd May	1944	British & Indian Troops seize Arakan.
28th May	1944	47 British POWs take part in the 'Great Escape' from Stalag Luft 111.
6th June	1944	D-Day Invasion of Normandy begins.
7th June	1944	D-Day+1, British troops capture Bayeux.
8th June	1944	D-Day+2, American troops capture Ste Mere Eglise.
9th June	1944	D-Day+3, Allies meet up in Normandy.
14th June	1944	First V1 Rockets fall on London, (V=Vergeltungswaffe).
15th June	1944	US Marines land on Saipan.
21st June	1944	First 1,000 Bomber Raid on Berlin.
3rd July	1944	Russian Troops recapture Minsk.
20th July	1944	Assassination attempt on Hitler by German Officers.
1st August	1944	Warsaw - Resistance fighters battle with German forces.
3rd August	1944	Germans leave Channel Islands.
16th August	1944	Canadian troops capture Falaise in Normandy.
25th August	1944	Paris liberated by Free French Troops.
3rd September	1944	Brussels liberated.
6th September	1944	Russian troops reach Yugoslavia.
8th September	1944	First V2 Rockets fall on London.
10th September	1944	Russian troops invade Bulgaria.
16th September	**1944**	**Wellington Bomber crashes into sea off St Bees Head - never found.**
19th September	1944	British Paratroopers drop on Arnhem in Holland.
26th September	1944	Remaining British Paratroopers withdrawn from Arnhem.
2nd October	1944	Germans leave Athens.
14th October	1944	Rommel commits suicide.
19th October	1944	Germans leave Belgrade.
27th October	1944	Kamikaze attacks on US ships in the Philippines.
2nd November	1944	Germans leave Greece.
11th November	**1944**	**Britain's Home Guard 'stood down'.**
12th November	1944	German Battleship Tirpitz sunk.
18th November	1944	US Troops enter Germany.
27th November	1944	Antwerp docks now open to Allies.
30th November	1944	American planes bomb Tokyo.
13th November	1944	Churchill celebrates his 70th birthday.
3rd December	**1944**	**Stand Down Parade of 4th,5th and 6th Battalions Home Guard at Workington.**
16th December	1944	New towns to be developed for Londoners.
16th December	1944	Battle of the Bulge in the Ardennes.
17th December	**1944**	**Workington's Beehive Co-op, Vulcans Lane, burnt to the ground-cost £55,000**
22nd December	1944	Bandleader Glen Miller missing on a flight to France.
3rd January	1945	Battle of the Bulge ends in defeat for Germans.
5th January	1945	US Marines capture Iwo-Jima

viii

12th January	1945	First 1,000 (US) Bomber raid on Berlin.
13th January	1945	Churchill, Roosevelt and Stalin end Yalta Conference.
23rd January	1945	RAF bombing causes a firestorm at Dresden.
7th March	1945	Allies capture the City of Cologne.
19th March	1945	Us troops capture Remagen Bridge over the Rhine.
22nd March	1945	Mandalay captured from Japanese, by British 14th Army.
22nd March	**1945**	**Workington man awarded George Medal, for saving blazing ammo train. (Bootle).**
2nd April	1945	Hitler and his new wife Eva Braun, commit suicide in the Berlin Bunker.
12th April	1945	Japanese battleship Yamato sunk by US fleet.
25th April	1945	US President F D Roosevelt dies, Harry S Truman takes over.
28th April	1945	US troops meet up with Russians on the Banks of the Elbe River.
30th April	1945	Mussolini & his mistress killed by partisans.
3rd May	1945	Russian army enters Berlin.
5th May	1945	Over 100 Japanese aircraft shot down over Okinawa.
7th May	1945	British troops capture Rangoon.
8th May	1945	Germany's Chief of Staff, General Alfred Jodl signs the surrender document.
8th May	**1945**	**Victory in Europe Day, (VE Day). West Cumbrian's celebrate.**
10th June	1945	Germany now divided into four occupation zones.
15th June	1945	Britain begins Demobilisation.
18th June	1945	Australian forces invade Borneo.
2nd July	1945	Posdam conference ends in disarray.
16th July	1945	London's West End lit up again. Nations Street lights turned on again.
17th July	1945	Prototype Atomic Bomb exploded at Los Alamos in the New Mexico Desert.
26th July	1945	Potsdam Conference Opens.
28th July	1945	Japan is told to surrender or face ' Prompt and Utter destruction.
31st July	1945	1,000 Carrier borne aircraft attack Japanese islands.
6th August	1945	US Aircraft bomb five Japanese Cities
9th August	1945	US drops Atomic Bomb on Hiroshima, 80,000 dead, 80,000 wounded.
14th August	1945	US drops second Atomic Bomb on Nagasaki 40,000 dead. 80,000 wounded.
14th August	1945	Japan agrees to 'unconditional surrender'.
15th August	1945	Victory over Japan Day, (VJ Day).
29th August	1945	Allied occupation of Japan begins.
12th September	1945	All Japanese Forces in South East Asia surrender.
19th September	1945	Britain to allow India Independence.
7th October	1945	First POW return from the Far East.
3rd November	1945	British dockers return to work after seven weeks strike.
13th November	1945	General Charles de Gaulle elected President of France.
16th November	1945	UNESCO founded.
20th November	1945	Nuremberg trials of top Nazis begin.
10th December	1945	Minimum daily wage in Britain set at ten shillings
21st December	1945	General George S Patton dies after car crash in Germany.
27th December	1945	International Monetary Fund (IMF) and World Bank set up.

Abbreviations & Glossary

AA	Anti-Aircraft
AFS	Auxiliary Fire Service
ARP	Air Raid Precautions
ATC	Air Training Corps
ATS	Auxiliary Territorial Service (women's section of the army)
BEF	British Expeditionary Force
CD	Civil Defence
CO	Conscientious Objector
CWAEC	County War Agricultural Executive Committee
DA	Delayed Action (bomb)
ENSA	Entertainment's National Service Association
EWO	Essential Work Order
EWS	Emergency Water Supply
HE	High Explosive
HG	Home Guard
IB	Incendiary Bomb
LDV	Local Defence Volunteer
LEA	Local Education Authority
M-O	Mass-Observation
MAP	Ministry of Aircraft Production
MOH	Medical Officer Of Health
MOI	Ministry of Information
MT	Motor Transport
NCO	Non Commissioned Officer
NFS	National Fire Service
POW	Prisoner of War
QL site	Nighttime Bombing Decoy
RAF	Royal Air force
RNAD	Royal Naval Armament Depot
RNAS	Royal Naval Air Station
ROC	Royal Observer Corps
ROF	Royal Ordnance Factory
SHQ	Squadron Headquarters
UXB	Unexploded Bomb
V1	German 'Vengeance' Rocket Mk1
V2	German 'Vengeance' Rocket MK2
VE	Victory in Europe Day
VJ	Victory over Japan Day
WAAF	Women's Auxiliary Air Force
WRENS	Women's Royal Naval Service
WLA	Women's Land Army
WVS	Women's Voluntary Service

CONTENTS

The Workington Keep 2

The Defended Localities 4

Workington's Defences 12

Auxiliary Forces 21

Farming 28

Working Life 34

Wartime Fund Raising 39

Maryport 45

Cockermouth 49

Whitehaven 50

Home Defence 62

Wartime Appeals 71

The Home Front 78

Wartime Industry 87

Distington 93

Bibliography 97

The Workington Keep

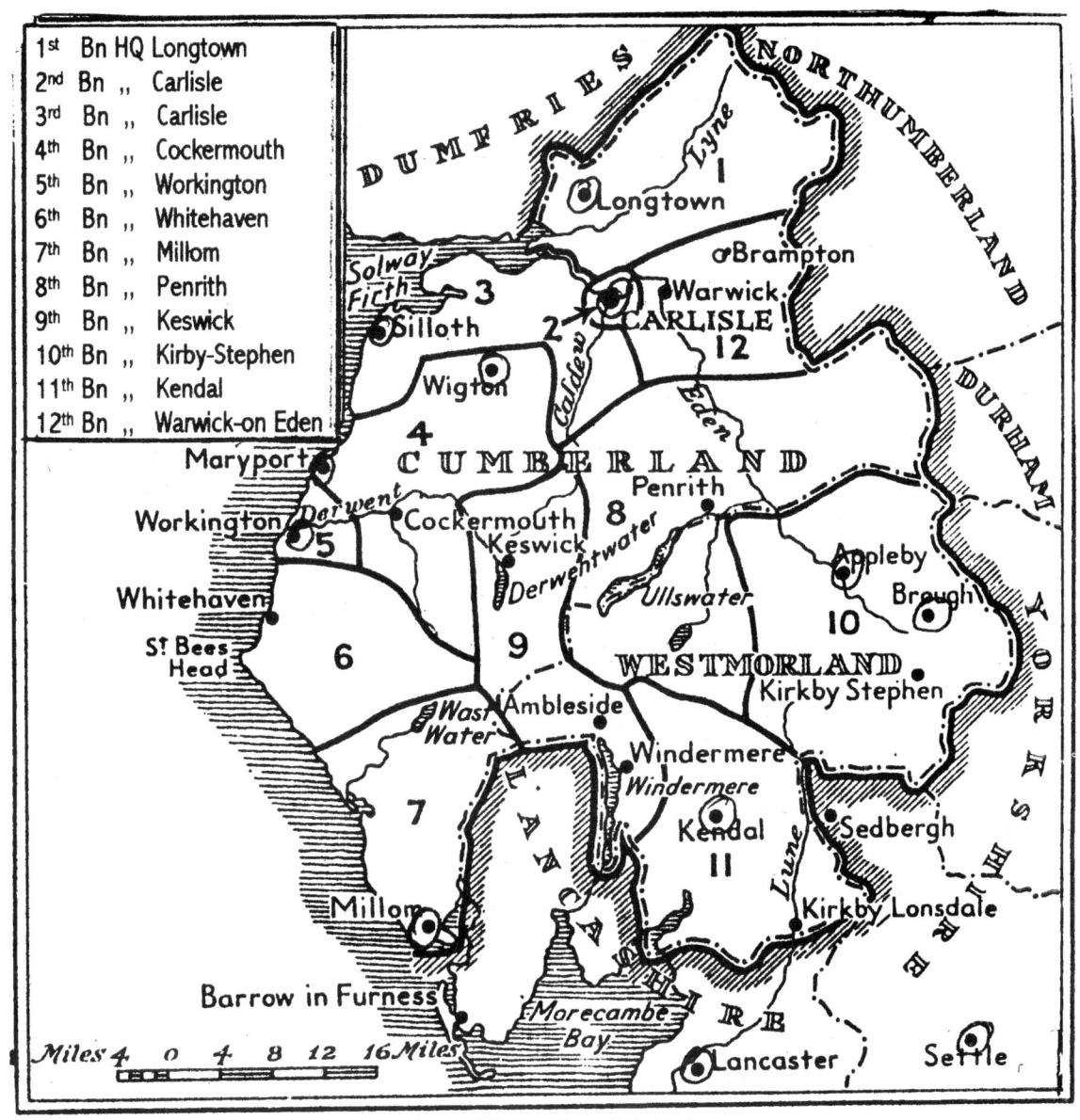

1st	Bn HQ	Longtown
2nd	Bn ,,	Carlisle
3rd	Bn ,,	Carlisle
4th	Bn ,,	Cockermouth
5th	Bn ,,	Workington
6th	Bn ,,	Whitehaven
7th	Bn ,,	Millom
8th	Bn ,,	Penrith
9th	Bn ,,	Keswick
10th	Bn ,,	Kirby-Stephen
11th	Bn ,,	Kendal
12th	Bn ,,	Warwick-on Eden

Location of Home Guard Battalions

Almost before Mr. Anthony Eden (the new Secretary of State for War) had finished his broadcast, the police station at Workington was under siege. Many who arrived were WW1 veterans, including one from Clifton, and one from Workington, each minus a leg. It was the 14th of May 1940; the Secretary of State had asked for Local Defence Volunteers (**LDV**) between the ages of 17 and 65.

This surge of manpower overwhelmed the recruiting officers, but somehow, names, occupations and addresses were taken. This was the core of men, which became, **The 5th (Cumberland) Battalion Home Guard**, (E. Group), affiliated to the Border Regiment. Indeed such was their pride in this gallant regiment, that the Home Guard wore the Borders Badge until they were stood down on December 3, 1944.

By 20th July 1940, the LDV had changed to the **'Home Guard'** simply because the PM Winston Churchill did not like the original cumbersome title. In 1944 the battalion strength was 104 officers and 1,679 other ranks.

Part of the defence of Workington and District was entrusted to these men under the command of Lt. Col. W.H. McCowan, CBE. DSO. succeeded later by Lt. Col G. T. Weir and his Second in Command Major E. G. Sarsfield-Hall CMG, (Ex Governor of Khartoum). They worked with some Regular Officers and men from the Border Regiment, namely Capt. E.J.B. Harrison who was appointed Adjutant; Capt. E. C. Peters became Quartermaster; Company Sergeant Major T. Heskett and CSM T. Payton permanent staff instructors.

Major EG Sarsfield-Hall. KMG.

Another regular unit of the Border Regiment (8th Batt) used Workington's drill hall in Edkin Street for messing, and the rest were based at Workington Hall. After many experiments, including the use of flying columns, para-shots, and small patrols, it was decided to concentrate the battalion on defending Workington as a nodal point, and if under attack, to fall back on an area called the **Marsh.** This stronghold was deemed to be the **KEEP**, while there was to be platoon strength, at **Defended Localities,** backed up by two "Flying Columns" each consisting of four battle platoons.

Later a Local Defence Committee was set up under Rear Admiral J.D.Campbell MVO. OBE. RN. SNO. Its members were Superintendent Ritchie, Commanding Officer of the Local Army unit, Lt. Col. G.T. Weir - Home Guard, Fire Brigade, OC the Coastal Battery and Mr. C.W. Murray-Civil Defence.

Stand Down, Col Dix-Perkins Inspecting HG.

The Defended Localities.

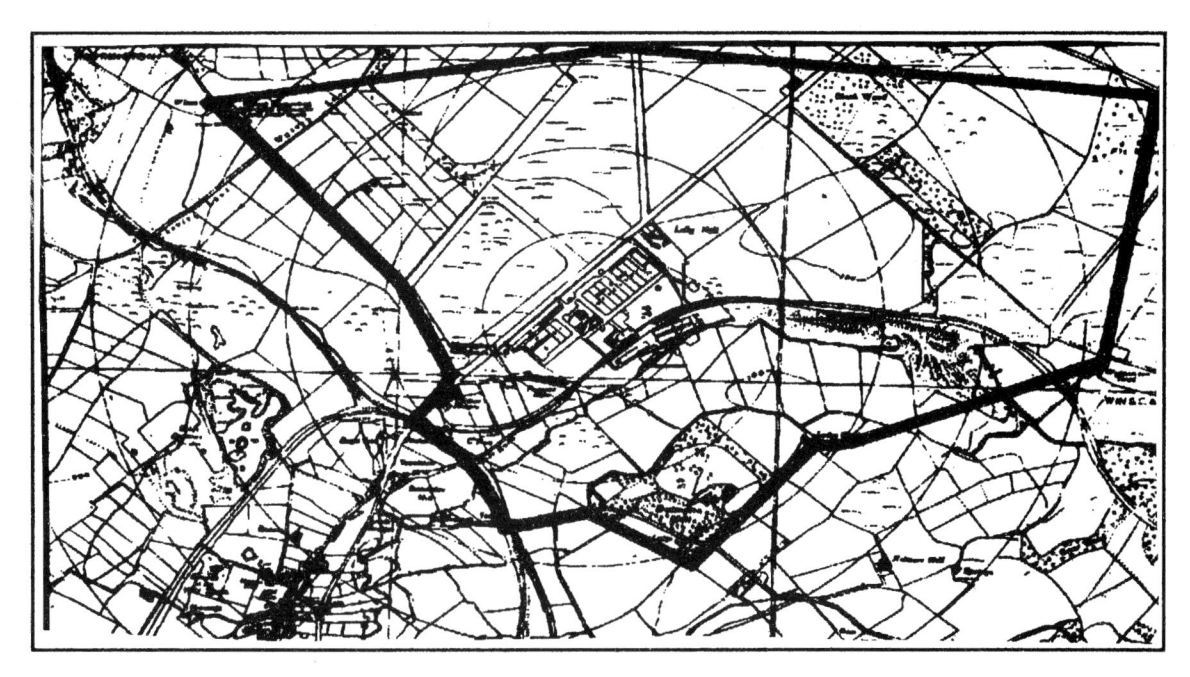

High Duty Alloys Defence Plan

- **High Duty Alloys Factory at Distington.**

This factory produced wrought aluminium alloys essential for the aircraft industry and one of the most vital and strategic in the area. This factory was protected by **"E" Company,** Home Guard drawn from employees, staff and some local men. They used Lilly Hall farm and the cottage, provided by Mr. D. H. Woodward, General Manager H.D.A for a HQ. This was turned into a guard house, four lecture rooms, storage space and an armoury.

The Defences were 8 Marlin Anti Aircraft Guns and 9 Hispano 20mm Anti Aircraft Guns clustered in batteries of threes, in strong 'Nests' inside the factory perimeter fence. Some of these men eventually became the **C troop L.A.A Royal Artillery** Area (M) Liverpool.

"E" Company was also responsible for road blocks on the Distington to Harrington road, as well as one on Workington road. Regular patrols were also made in the areas from Whinns Reservoir, Black Wood, Windscales and Distington Hall. The Bomb Disposal Squad under Lt. F. E. Ansell operated with this company.

Later in a 1946, In a 'Now it can be told' talk to the local Rotary club, it was revealed that this unit had a secret section, which consisted of 'nominated women.' They had done night guards to spell the men off and had 'assisted' in collecting information, during the Inter platoon and company's mock battles.

- **Workington Iron and Steel Works, (WISCo) Moss Bay Works.**

The primary defence was two pill boxes, one on the south end of slag bank, the other on Moss Bay Road. These and the shore line to the pier, was the responsibility of "**A" Company** Home Guard, drawn from steelworks personnel, and later some from the Distington Haematite and Iron Works (Later D.E.C).

As a further precaution a line of slag moulds, (known as skulls) were tipped from ladles on to the shore line to act as Anti Tank Traps, protecting the rear of the works, and Workington's Shore Terrace area. The Steel Works - or "Combine" -as it was known locally, operated the largest electric steel furnace in Britain for the Ministry of Supply, producing high grade steel for ball and roller bearings and billets for steel munitions.

Anti-Tank Traps-Salterbeck Shore.

Piquet's and patrols were mounted, and later no less than 18. Hispano 20mm Anti -Aircraft Guns, operated by regular troops of the **Royal Artillery**, were deployed around the works and its slag banks, along with 4 spigot Mortars, 4 Browning medium Machine Guns, and 2 Northover Projectors.

This with the small arms issued, e.g., 12 Browning Automatic Rifles, 161, American.300 Rifles. 3 Boys Anti Tank Guns, 109 Sten Guns made the company one of the most heavily armed. This had not always been the case, as in early 1940 the "Combine's" wagon shop had made wooden rifles for the LDF, the 'real' weapons were rather late in being issued. After Dunkirk, many heavy weapons were handed back to allow the army to re-equip, for the expected invasion.

The Defence Officer at the steel works was the redoubtable Major-General, S. B. Pope CB, DSO (ex Dunkirk), aided by Capt. Moffatt. New premises were built inside the works, which contained a HQ, barrack room, armoury, and office, built at a cost of £3,259, a.22 rifle range was included.

'**A' Company** was organized into four units -Day Workers - Steel Workers-Blast Furnacemen and Dock Workers. It had a very good record for attendance at parades, with full wages being paid to any NCOs or men who attended training with regular army units.

A Coy Shooting Team

In 1944 the company re-organized as Anti Aircraft gunners, taking over from the Royal Artillery, using the Hispano guns, sited around the works, with aeroplanes sent over twice a week for 'eye' shooting. Home Guard duties were tailored to the men's shift patterns and they were later paid 3/- per night for a 'inlying' picket. This company also provided the battalion's fife & drum band, under Corporal L. Lee, with Sergeant R. Ryan as drum major. Because the Works was a large target for the German bombers that flew mainly at night, production stopped at 4pm. The coke ovens were roofed over and the large Bessemer converters were screened, to prevent discovery by the bombers.

Two Decoy Sites were also used (type QL & QF) one was situated in a field at Siddick, and the other at Moresby Moss. Both were of the nighttime type, and were designed so that if the works were under attack, lights and fires would appear a these remote locations. Apparatus would mimic locomotive fire boxes, open doors, and furnace glare, thus confusing the enemy bomb aimers and encouraging them to bomb the decoy site. Both sites had a control room, with civilian staff, and generators (powered by Morris Cowley engines), being sand bagged and covered in earth (Revetment). Fortunately they were not subjected to attack, however nationally as many bombs fell on these sites, as fell on the intended targets. These sites were inspired by Colonel Turner's department at the Shepperton film studios, the same unit made inflatable Sherman tanks and dummy aircraft for the War Office.

Decoy Site-Control Room-Siddick.

• The Railways and the upper Town
Were protected by men of **"C" company,** Home Guard, drawn from the staff of the London Midland and Scottish Railway (LMS), along with men from the Cumberland Motor Services, Post Office, and staff of the Corporation Gas and Electricity Utility. They patrolled the centre of town, Workington Bridge, Calva Junction Signal box, Derwent Railway Bridge, Annie Pit Lane, Fisher St and Hagg Hill, armed with rifles and Sten guns, along with machine guns placed at strategic locations: their HQ (the store rooms at Central Station), And the Pill Box at Castle gardens. Reserves of men were stationed in the Princess Hall.

• The Keep and Lower Town
The responsibility of the men of **"B" Company**, Company Commander Major GT Weir,(Later Major CA Donnithorne, DCM). They also acted as one of the flying columns. HQ was located in the Hippodrome Ballroom, underneath the cinema.

This had tragic consequences one evening when some live bullets became mixed up with some blank .303 bullets. A single round was discharged from a rifle, through the ballroom roof, coming out of the floor of the cinema above seriously wounding a woman seated in the cinema, in the leg.

Among the company duties were long hours in the look out station on the shore, along with eight patrols of four men, that were sent out nightly, each covering between 8/10 miles. The final strength was 18 officers, and 358 other Ranks, including "B" Mobile Company.

Armaments included 1 anti-tank gun, 2, 6 Spigot mortars, 4 Browning medium machine guns, 9 Browning automatic rifles, 24 EY rifles, 196 rifles, 6 anti tank rifles and 124 Sten guns.

• Harrington, Shore & Shore Works

Protected by five platoons of **"F" Company**, commanded by Major J. Lister, Second in Command, Capt. R. Hyde, Company Training Officer Lt. JC Andrews, CQMS Lt. JW Beresford, Intelligence Officer Lt. DH Jessop. Platoon Commanders 2Lt J Boal, 2Lt RJ Harkness, Lt. M Newton, Lt. WE Reed, Lt. J Weir and Lt. J Carruthers.

Based in the old school room on Church Road, they protected the works, occupied the pillbox at Copperas Hill, patrolled Victoria Sq., Rose Hill, Archer St, Harrington Parks Farm, and the road block situated at the junction of Lime road and Lowca road.

Stanton Shelter, Rose Hill, Harrington.

WW2 Nissen Hut, High Harrington.

Weapon practice was carried out on a 30 yard range, constructed on property owned by the Harrington Shore Works, obtained through the works Defence Officer, Lt. Beaumont (Regular Army). These men also had the largest area to patrol.

Company strength was approximately, 10 Officers, and 198 Other Ranks, weapons issued included 2 Spigot mortars, 6 Browning automatic rifles, 15 E.Y. Rifles, 70 Sten guns and 3 Northover Projectors.

• The Clifton, St. Helens Mines and Thermal Syndicate Factory

Defended by "**D**" **Company** from their HQ at Clifton Lodge, there was a platoon at each works location. Most of the recruits were from the West Cumberland mines and had considerable local knowledge. This was put to good use in the many exercises they took part in, with regular troops, who were 'captured' every time. Probably because of the semi commando training two of the platoons, had undertaken. On one hazardous river crossing exercise, carried out on the River Derwent, Lieut. Houghton got into difficulties but was hauled out of the water, by Pte. R. Logan, who was later awarded the Commander-in Chief's Certificate of Merit.

Officers from D Company.

First Company commander was Captain T. Tomlinson (a WW1 Company Commander). After his death in 1942, Capt., J.G. Chicken took over, and Lieut. B.J. Smallwood was promoted Second-in Command. Platoon Commanders were 2/Lt J. Jenkinson, Lt. TA Dixon, Lt. T. Crellin, Lt. W. McKeating, Lt. FT Hodgson, 2/Lt G. Lamont, Lt. P. Patterson, Lt. A Hayes and 2/Lt RS Lyall (Thermal syndicate).

Later the static defence was discontinued, and the company formed a mobile column under Capt. TG McKeating, consisting of motor cycle out-riders, cars and buses. The company had some of the best marksmen. A very good social life existed, along with a Rugby Team, social club, vegetable shows, a concert party, and a battalion band formed out of the Great Clifton Prize Band.

The Company consisted of 11 officers and 256 other ranks. Among its armaments were two water cooled Browning medium machine guns, also two strange pieces of ordnance called Smiths guns. The latter was a private enterprise weapon, produced by the firm of Trianco, expressly for home defence, and was made to be pulled behind a private car, if no military transport was available.

HQ Company 5ᵀʰ Battalion HG.

HQ Staff 1940

Signal Section

- **Battalion HQ**

Commanded by Major H.V. Lancaster, Second in Command Capt. J. Kirkbride, was situated at the Tuscan Villa and Wesleyan Hall, both situated on Fisher St. It was here that the intelligence section under Capt. W. Fletcher the medics, Dr. R. E. Fletcher and Major T.T. Graham, Signals-Lt. T. Fletcher, liaison, clerks, women auxiliaries and drivers and Armourer Sgt. J. Milburn BEM., were based, all reporting to the CO and his staff.

The Headquarters Staff had two main tasks.
1. Maintain communications with battalion in an emergency.
2. Collate through the Intelligence section, all information of military value.

Among its resources were two dispatch riders, 45, portable wireless sets, 1 C58 long range set, a pigeon signal service, and a red van called 'Old Faithful.'

A 4" BL MkVII gun of the Workington Battery

- **Shore Battery.**

Consisted of two, 4 inch BL MkVII naval guns in a concrete and steel emplacement, complete with an engine house. Outside were electrically controlled rocket projectors, backed up by two Lewis machine guns and a giant search-light for night shooting. This battery was under the command of regular troops from the **406 (Workington) Battery**, of the **561 Coast Regiment, Royal Artillery**. Commanded by Maj. G.D. Copley

Turret interior.

later Major W. W. Oates, RA. and consisted of 17 regulars, aided by over 34 officers and men of the Home Guard, under Lt. R.G. Lawson (ex WW1 Pilot), Sgt. Major GS Goss, Sgt. WH Bayliff and Lance/ Sgt. A Hall.

These men also trained as an Infantry Unit, to protect the battery from land attack, they eventually wore the Royal Artillery cap badge, the red and blue "flash," and the white lanyard over the right shoulder, and were some of the most dedicated and skilled shots amongst the Coastal batteries.

Many attended training courses at the R.A. Coast Artillery School at Llandudno in North Wales and on occasions the Home Guard Gunnery unit, visited the coastal batteries at Barrow. Taking part in naval and anti-tank shoots against moving targets using 75mm. Field guns. Tank "busting" was also carried out at Workington against sea targets with 75mm weapons.

Group of Workington Coastal Gunners (HG).

Workington's Defences.

Pill Box-Type 22-Copperas Hill.

Invasion precautions were, pill boxes, one in the front room of the toll bar house at the junction of Calva Brow and Workington Bridge. On the bridge itself was a road barrier of the knife edge type, aided by concrete blocks. The same set-up was also in use at the Junction of Northside road and the railway bridge. Other Pill Boxes and barriers were situated at Castle Gardens, Mossbay, Siddick (alongside the St. Helens Railway Bridge), Cuckoo Arch, and a solitary Pill box (type 22), that still remains in good condition at Copperas Hill overlooking the sea at Harrington. Parts of the coast were also sown with land mines.

Workington Hall

The Hall had originally been earmarked as a dormitory for some of the pupils and masters of Mill Hill school who were due to be evacuated from London in 1939. The Halls owner Mrs. Chance of "Homeacres", Carlisle, had already spent £350 on refurbishment, but the school was accommodated at St. Bees, sharing a class room with the public school.

Eventually the Military took over the Hall, the first unit being the **5th battalion of the Border Regiment**. Victor O'Connor and his 'marras' were already in the TA. When War was declared, they mustered at Whitehaven's drill hall and marched the eight miles along the road to Workington Hall.

Once settled in, they took up guard duties and mounted pickets at locations that included Armthwaite Hall, Ouse Bridge and the RNAD at Broughton Moor.

However it was not long before they met the Halls most famous resident-a ghost called **'Galloping Harry'**. First, a sentry fainted with fright, then Sergeant Major Leck reeled into the mess, ashen faced; it had passed him on the back stairs! For it was here that Harry had been slain by his French maid, who had killed him by dragging him downstairs by his heels, his head hitting every step on the way. She then propped him up in bed, and made her getaway after robbing the Hall. The back stairs were assiduously avoided by the troops after dark, from then on.

The 5th Batt, was then split into the 7th and both went off to combat postings. Next it was the turn of the 8th battalion (HD) later to be re-numbered the 30th (HD) battalion under Lieutenant R. Strong MC. and CSM Robinson DCM. MM. A high proportion of the battalion was over 45 years of age and some were WW1 veterans. However fresh duties included guarding the RADAR stations on St. Bees Head and Barrow (the docks and petrol depot), aerodromes at Silloth and Kirkbride, two satellite landing grounds at Hutton and Hornby Hall, and also the ammunition dump at Longtown. However, in March 1942 their role was changed and men from the **Cheshire Regiment** took over.

The troops guarding the Hall came under attack on Easter Saturday 1940 at 10pm, and military discipline was sorely put to the test. Cries of 'who goes there' echoed around the 'blacked out' Hall, bayonets were fixed and the troops assumed the 'on Guard position.'

In the blackout loomed a large unruly mob intent on crossing the picket line - it was the **Uppies and Downies** football game on their way to 'Hail' the ball.

By all accounts it was a game to remember; the ball had been in the river twice, the beck five times, the cricket field and allotments were again, trampled underfoot, and

Uppies & Downies Game, 1940.

for good measure as the crowd of about two hundred burst through the small gate leading to the Hall Grounds. A disused coal house collapsed on top of the scrum, leaving a few with broken limbs and cuts. On seeing the troops with bayonets fixed, what was later described in the local paper, as an 'Irish Parliament' took place, who was going up to 'Hail' the ball? In the end, they all 'hailed 'it, the military were overcome, and Horace Bell of Darcy Street was said to have tossed the ball into the air three times, and was thus deemed to have hailed the ball.
After the main body of ball players had dispersed to local inns and taverns, covered in coal dust, the ambulance and military first aid teams treated the wounded, running out of bandages in the process. A result was later declared, of *Troops 0, Uppies 1,*

Drill Hall Edkin St

Originally the Headquarters of 51st Regiment Artillery (TA), for the 203 and 204 batteries, they had spent the summer of '39 at a firing camp in Wales, practicing with 45 Howitzers and Rapid fire AA guns, but were then called to fight with the BEF in France.

After the initial call for volunteers, many drill parades were held for the LDV. Almost every evening, groups in civilian clothes learned foot drill, and for many weeks no uniforms or weapons were issued. However the police had shotguns, revolvers and some rifles which were placed on loan to the LDV. Later the wooden rifles made at the WISC were used for drill. An issue of bottles filled with a compound of petrol, tar and resin known as 'Molotov Cocktails' was also received; these had allegedly proved a success in the Spanish civil war, when used against tanks.

There was a delivery from the United States (June 1940), of Ross .300 calibre rifles, these were made to a 1912 British design. They arrived in crates of twelve, all embedded in hard yellow grease, covering the volunteers who opened the ammunition boxes and unpacked them. Tin openers were used on the ammo boxes

Workington Drill Hall.

that gave off a smell similar to pear drops when opened. All together 832 Ross rifles were issued, along with 48 powerful Browning automatic rifles, along with large quantities of pattern 36 grenades.

In June and July 1940, khaki denim uniforms arrived and eventually all were equipped with cloth battledress, anklets, boots, overcoats, gas capes, gas masks, eye shields, steel helmets, belts and frogs, pouches, haversacks, anti-gas ointment, field dressings and personal weapons.

Later "B" company HQ, was based at the Officers Mess in the Drill Hall, but had to move out when Lt. Colonel McDonald arrived with the 8th battalion of the Border Regiment.

WEAPONS ISSUED TO THE BATTALION

Weapons	Totals	A Coy Steel Co	B Coy Town	C Coy Upper Town	D Coy Clifton Siddick	E Coy HDA	F Coy Harrington	HQ Coy Town
2 Pdr. Anti-Tank Guns	4	1		1	2			
Smith Guns	5		2	1	2			
Spigot Mortars	22	4	6	4		6	2	
Browning Machine Guns	19	4	4	2	2	7		
Browning Automatic Rifles	48	12	9	6	6	9	6	
Rifles EY. Discharger Cup	105	24	24	18	9	15	15	
Rifles Ross, .300	832	161	196	125	105	118	93	34
Rifles .22	16	3	3	2	3	3	2	
Boys Anti-Tank Rifles	19	3	6	3	4	3		
Sten Guns	575	109	124	97	61	91	70	23
Lewis Guns	3			1	1			1
Northover Projectors	11	2	2	2	2		3	
Marlin Anti-Aircraft M.Gs	8					8		
Hispano Anti-Aircraft M.Gs	27	18				9		

The Blacker Bombard (Spigot Mortar) Manned by the HG.

20mm. Hispano Anti-Aircraft Machine Gun.

Home Guard Troops with a Browning Machine Gun.

Home Guard, Manning a Northover Projector.

Home Guard, Loading a Smiths Gun.

Regular Troops with a 2 Pounder Anti-Tank Gun.

Troops with Ross Rifles.

Troops with a Boys Anti-Tank Gun.

Tugs in the Prince of Wales Dock.

Docks & Harbour

Steel, Iron ore, timber and general cargo, including 300 WACO American gliders, flowed through the Port and two old Wooden Steamers took munitions out. General cargo was also handled, and items as diverse as shoes, cars and boots all loaded under the watchful eye of Horace Green the master stevedore, or Lt 'Taff' Banks RN. On the river side of the harbour, a powerful Air Sea Rescue Launch remained in readiness, (for 6 months) as there were numerous plane crashes in the sea, especially North of Maryport near the coastal training airfields. It was later transferred to Kircudbright.

HMS Chatteden Unloading.

HMS Chatteden, With Armed Guard.

Supervising the naval and military aspects of the Port was Captain Greenhow, and Capt. Bunfield (Army). A coastal battery and machine guns protected the approach to the port, as well as two electrically controlled mines set each side of the channel entrance, the controls, of which were in the look-out station.

The port channel had to be kept clear so the floating unit of Dredger (Lord Joicey), two hoppers and tug boat were used; the manning of these was considered, a 'perk' as the men received 'sea going' rations. There were numerous incidents for the Harbour Master, Captain Thompson to handle. The ship 'Towerfield' was stranded on Northside shore and broke its back and it was towed into the dock after Drummonds engineers had carried out emergency repairs. Then it sank onto the concrete bottom of the Dock and after a diver had cleared the coal bunkers, the ship realigned itself. It was then repaired with large riveted fish plates, and sailed away for more permanent repairs.

Workington Docks, Captain S Caravick, Master of the Chatteden.

The Royal Naval Armaments Depot
Broughton Moor (The Dump). A large storage and inspection site built in 1938, guarded by Ministry of Defence police, regulars and often a local Home Guard unit from Seaton or Broughton Moor.

Some munitions were delivered by road, but most came by rail via Seaton Junction and Camerton, straight into the depot's sidings, where it was transferred to the small 30 inch, gauge railway. The small wagons were hauled by either **Ruston** or **Hunslet** diesel locomotives to some of the 500 buildings (many underground) on the large site. This complex had over 15 miles of roads on the extensive 1,200 acre site. An overflow storage facility was employed in the tunnels and kilns of the nearby Camerton Brickworks.

The Depot also had its decoy site at the disused Alice Pit. This was of the QL type, designed to burst into flames and show lights if the 'Dump' was under attack at night, similar to the ones at Moresby Moss and St. Helens (Siddick).

Tragedy struck in January 1944, a weak fuse on a mortar bomb that was part of the Naval anti -submarine 'hedgehog' system, exploded in the general purpose laboratory No 3. This set off a 'sympathetic' explosion of over half a ton of bombs in a railway wagon nearby.

The blast was heard fifteen miles away, six feet thick concrete walls were damaged, and unfortunately, eleven civilian workers (mostly women) were killed, and a further thirty-nine had minor injuries. Two days later, a naval rating returned home on leave late at night, and getting no answer at his house, made his way to the Social Club, where a fund-raising event for the victims and relatives of the disaster was being held. Later he was told by a senior officer that his wife had been one of those killed. This was the only major accident during wartime on the site.

The Royal Observer Corps
The Royal Observer Corps, (founded in 1925); the Workington post, number 32/F.3; opened in October 1939, was sited at Hawk Hill Seaton.

Operated by volunteers who, at first, wore civilian clothes with a distinguishing arm band (Brassard). Later they were issued with RAF style uniform, but with a different rank structure,(a Chief Observer equalled an Army Sergeant in Rank). **S**ome were eventually paid £3 for a 48 hour week. The beret badge was the beacon firelighter, their motto **'Forewarned is Forearmed.'**

The site was operated 24 hours a day, with three on duty at anyone time. The height, speed and range of all aircraft, were plotted by a Mk11A Instrument with a Micklethwaite height correction attachment, which projected the sighting on to a 6-8 mile great circle map of the area. These details and numbers of enemy aircraft were then telephoned to 32 Air Group at Carlisle and also from similar ROC sites at Allonby, Cockermouth and Whitehaven.

A Typical ROC Post.

The Post was later equipped with flares to warn of imminent attack, and help damaged or lost 'friendly' aircraft (on demand), duties that earned them the title, "The Eyes and Ears of the RAF."

Auxiliary Forces

Police

Britain needed over 130,000 more police officers to cope with the effects of war, and the new powers given to them by Parliament; it effectively meant that we had a national force.

The Chief Constable of Cumberland and Westmorland, Mr. MPB Browne, solved the personnel shortage in four stages.

- **First Police Reserve** - Retired elderly officers were asked to volunteer for duty. Many lasted for only six months because of long hours and the physical stress involved.

- **Police War Reservists -** men in reserved occupations up to the age of 35 were allowed to join, and generally had minimum training.

- **The Women's Police Corps -** Usually only "allowed" to provide clerical support, staff canteen work, and clean / prepare vehicles.

- **Special Constables** - One of the most valuable groups in Cumberland. (Over 1,451) They were usually farmers, publicans, and others who knew the land and the local populace; anything abnormal in the countryside was quickly noted and investigated.

Much extra police work was taken up with lighting restrictions, aliens, testing for 'red' petrol and offences against military law.
Workington's police Superintendent was W. Ritchie, assisted by Five Sergeants and 15 Constables.

Fire Brigade

The brigade was soon supplemented by men of the **Auxiliary Fire Service** (AFS) who outnumbered the regulars' 10-1, however there was some friction at large stations, as the regular fire fighters resented the volunteers, whose pay nearly rivalled their own.

Mr. W. Charters, the fire brigade captain, needed extra resources, so the purchase of a 26hp Nash saloon, for £50, a Bedford bus for use as a hose carrier at £75, and a covered trailer at £15, were welcome additions to the fleet, as was a wheeled Fire escape. The Harrington Road fire station was becoming too small, so plans were put in hand for new premises in the town.
Then another change occurred, the **National Fire Service** (NFS) was formed. It had been found that during the London "Blitz", and the heavy bombings of other cities, that when many fire brigades became involved, chaos often resulted. Ranks, words of command and messages were not standardized, and sometimes apparatus would not fit another brigade's hydrants!

Out of the 1,665 Local Authorities who had been organizing fire brigades, the NFS replaced them with less than 50 Fire Forces operating under one unified control.
The new post of Britain's 'Chief of Fire Staff' was held by the appropriately-named Sir Aylmer Firebrace, who had been so successful as the Regional Fire Officer for London, during the Blitz.
Many AFS men were eventually recruited in preference to regulars, and Workington NFS was now expanded. The Leader Mr J. Drabble NFS Liaison officer for the area, held regular meetings with Sector Captains, Party leaders and Fire Guards. Sub-stations were established at Drummonds on the Marsh, Salterbeck, and Duke St., with the brigades' workshops in Gordon's Garage, Washington Street.

The largest fire they attended during the war was the Beehive Co-op in Vulcan's Lane when, during the Friday lunch break, on the 22nd December 1944, the whole block was burnt down. Workington Brigade was assisted by Whitehaven, Maryport and Cockermouth Brigades, and the fire was so intense that houses on the opposite side of the street had scorched front doors and cracked windows. First on the scene were some Burma veterans, who saved the stock of the boot and shoe department, then PC Johnstone braved the fire to rescue the £300 float and ledgers from the grocery dept. Miss Bernard the Bakery Manageress, who lived next door, had to vacate her house. This was the most extensive fire in the town for 22years, and the cost was estimated at £52,000.

Each commercial establishment had to have its fire watching and fire fighting team similar to the street fire parties. In all there were over 600 of these, 3,000 personnel signed up for duty in Workington town. Various small rivers were dammed and large tanks placed around the town, to provide Emergency Water Supplies,(**EWS**), the largest being in St. Michael's churchyard.

Women Auxiliaries
Were inspired by Dr. Edith Summerskill, MP. She had formed a body of women in London, who were trained to look after themselves in case of invasion.
The initial local meeting was arranged by Miss E. Short SRN,SGM, Superintendent Nursing Sister of the WISCo, at Moss Bay works, with about 180 women employees. It was decided to form a Women's Auxiliary Unit on the works, and agreed that:-

- Ranks should be-Section Leader, Deputy Leader, and Member.

- Each Department, having over 25 Volunteers, should be called a section, and have Section and Deputy leaders in charge.

- Training should be given in:-
Rifle Shooting (.22)	Signalling and Phonograms
Physical Training	First Aid
Cooking	Clerical Duties
Staffing of Home Guard HQ.	

They became "Home Guard Women Auxiliaries" who were issued with plaque brooches, bearing the letters "HG." No uniforms were ever issued, as the War Office declined to provide these.

Miss Short was in command, and every company wanted a WA section. They provided an invaluable service, staffed the Battalion HQ on all tactical schemes, took over telephones, managed clerical work, wrote up war and intelligence diaries, cooked, became transport drivers, and checked in stores day and night.
In addition they were also very good 'Shots' and a team consisting of Mrs. E. Hucknall, and the Misses E. Short, K. Weir, K. Wall, V. Bond, I. Day, A. Valentine, S. Harris, and W. Darby won six out of seven matches and were runners up to Colchester, in the National Inter-Unit Small Bore Rifle League Championship.

Workington Hospital
Two new wards had been built, one for women and a maternity unit. Sadly it had just lost one of it most loyal servants, Dr McKerrow who had died after giving the hospital 53 years service.

One of the busiest wards was the Accident department, which dealt with practically all wartime conditions. There were more industrial injuries, caused by full employment, long hours and road accidents, especially during the 'blackout' there was also a large increase in shipping traffic through the 'safe port'. So many nationalities were being treated that language cards were printed and issued to sailors. The Children's ward was also at full capacity, with the refugees requiring treatment. Fortunately help was at hand, with Red Cross nurses assisting, replacing many full-time nurses who were away on war service. Then in 1945 specialist treatment became available from Carlisle.

Civilian Measures
On October 27, 1940, Workington lost its sense of isolation, it was bombed !

The first air raid caused little damage as the explosives fell over the Merchants Quay and the abandoned Oldside Ironworks. Later during the night of November 29, 1940 there was another bombing raid which resulted in two houses at the bottom of Walker and Poole Road being damaged by an incendiary bomb, Afterwards there was a mental 'tightening of belts,' and military and civil defence affairs were given more respect; the 'phoney war' was now over.

Up to now the **Blackout Precautions**, to household windows, car headlights, and even bike lamps, were enforced by the Air Raid Precaution (**A.R.P**) Wardens. They also had responsibility for ambulances, shelters, home fire fighting equipment (and the provision of Special Constables). It had proved irksome, to the civilians, but now following these random raids, the grumbling stopped.

What the public did not realize was that in mid 1935 the government had asked all

Dornier Bomber used in the Barrow Raids.

local authorities to prepare air-raid precaution plans. Workington was well prepared. In the first World War over 1,400 people in Britain had been killed by bombs; it was apparent that more casualties would be caused in any future conflict.

However, the local community still had problems, for there was no petrol for private transport. Only doctors and officials had a petrol ration; even the steelworks official car, an Armstrong Siddeley was powered by gas produced from the coke works on the 'Combine'. This was stored on top of the car's roof, in a large unruly, floppy, gas bag.

This, along with food rationing, clothing rationing, and a points system for furniture,

Hienkel 111 Bomber.   Regulars over West Cumberland.

having to carry an identity card and a gas mask, the blackout, hundreds of evacuee's in towns and villages (billeting allowance 10/6d (52p) a week for a single child), having your Iron/steel railings & gates, taken for scrap, the dig for victory campaign, and the posting of loved ones overseas, (over 9,000 West Cumbrians, were in the forces) was accepted as part of the difficult but everyday scene.

Somehow, a spirit of togetherness was forged, long remembered by local people, who experienced those austere and dangerous times. For dangerous as it was, West Cumberland lost over 78 persons, to "WAR WORK" alone.

Deep Shelters were provided under Mandale's store, 16/18 Oxford St, in the cellar of the Albert hall, underneath Armstrong's fresh fish shop in Gordon St, the cellar of the United Club Portland Sq. and under Ambrose Palmer's paint store in Uldale St., the cellar of Chirnside's store in Gordon St and in cellars of various public houses. There was room for 2,215 people in these deep shelters - 7% of the town's population.

Surface Shelters - Aprox 47 were built in Workington. Builders were Lovell Bros., R. W. Copeland, and WA Walker, with a further 30 built by Gilmore and sons.

Warden's Posts - were situated at Marsh Side, the ambulance station in Vulcan's lane, Princess St., Gladstone St., Tarn St., at the rear of Moss-Bay Hotel, Annie Pit, Wetheriggs Rd, the Oval and Church Rd Harrington.

At Harrington, the Head Warden was Mr J. Knowles, with Deputy Wardens G. Pinkney and H. Simon, Ambulance warden Mr R. Blair; veterinary Warden Mr R. Ramsey.
Divisional Controller was Mr. CW Murray. Senior wardens, telephonists and training, were all located at the ARP Control Centre Stoneleigh, Cross hill. It was here that training in anti-gas, first aid and decontamination took place.

ARP Wardens Lamp.

Municipal Café - Oxford St. (Part of the British Restaurants) formerly Thomas Mandales showroom, was converted to a communal feeding centre at a cost of £2,750, It had professional kitchens fitted, and when opened in 1941, supplied a basic meal for the townsfolk.

You could still eat unrationed food in commercial restaurants at a price not exceeding 5/-, but it was illegal to serve more than two main courses, with the same meal.

The Café was self-service from a hatch, and provided a simple, filling meal for 10d or 1/- per person. Over 2,160 of these were opened up nation-wide, funded by local authorities on a non-profit making basis, but were guaranteed by the government. They were also used for training 'wartime' cooks. Troops home on leave, used the Café, and the canteen and recreation area at St. Johns Court, which contained games

& reading rooms, and also a refreshment area, run by members of the town's Free Churches.

Workington's MP Mr Tom Cape, speaking at the divisional Labour Party's annual meeting, in 1940 (his 22nd), before an audience of delegates from the mines, transport workers, steelworkers, railwaymen and trade unionists from the districts said "We are better equipped now than in March nineteen forty, and soon we will be able to cope with the Nazi war machine in all directions".

He then outlined details of the means test, and concluded his speech by saying *"I would remind you that some of the democratic rights may have to be set aside. You still have the right to criticise. Remember that you are in the greatest struggle that this country has been engaged in through-out history, and when some things may not come up to expectation, ask yourselves this; well under the circumstances, could anything better have been done?"*

Mr Tom Cape MP

Resolutions were then passed, one deploring the BBC, which had refused to use some artists and broadcasters, who did not share the corporation's own political views.

Enemy Aliens

Nationally in 1939, a large number of **NAZI** supporters and left wing refugees were 'rounded up' some billeted on a Surrey racecourse.

All other aliens went before tribunals, which classified them according to risk. Class 'A' was interned, class 'B' was restricted in their movements, class 'C' were set free. On 16/17th May 1940, all class 'B' aliens near vulnerable coastal areas were interned in great haste and secrecy. Most were given no time to put their affairs in order.
National newspapers whipped up public opinion, with slogans such as 'Intern the Lot,' many employers sacked foreigners and some local authorities turned them out of council houses.

Likewise, when Italy entered the War there were attacks on Italian restaurants and ice cream parlours; 4,000 Italians with less than 20 year's residence in Britain were then interned.
On the 10th, June 1940, even some category 'C' aliens who were under suspicion, were also interned. Those that were left were subject to a curfew, had restrictions

26

placed on travel, and were not allowed to own a bicycle, car or a map, without permission.

Most internees passed through squalid tented camps or disused old mills. Men and Women were kept separate before being shipped to the **IOM**, where some were eventually sent to the Dominions.

This stopped after the internee ship the **SS "Arandora Star"** was torpedoed, 300 miles north west of Ireland, by Captain Gunther Prien in U47 with great loss of life, on the 2nd, July 1940. A graphic account of this incident was provided by 21 year old Tom Lucas of Lowther Rd, The Ginns, Whitehaven. Tom had been a assistant steward on the elderly liner when it was torpedoed. Apparently the German and Italian internees had fought amongst themselves, up-turning lifeboats in the process. Tom had been picked up by a lifeboat containing some of the ship's crew. After many hours, supplies were dropped to them by a Sunderland flying boat; later they were picked up by a Canadian destroyer.

Locally, the courts were very harsh on aliens. A commercial traveller used the Green Dragon regularly in Portland Square. He had left Russia when he was three years old, but on two occasions had signed the guest book with different names. On one occasion he used the name Stienberg, and another time the anglicised name Shaw; the magistrates made an example of him, and the fine was £15. (£75 today).

Miners

The pits still working included Risehow, Gillhead, St. Helens, Solway, Aspatria, Clifton, Siddick, Camerton and Birkby.

On outbreak of war there were 15 active collieries in the area, operated by nine companies. The capacity was two million saleable tons of coal, with 4 pits producing 75% of the total.

Miners were now falling foul of the Ministry of Labour and National Service. Absenteeism was being reported, and
miners were being jailed on a regular basis. One young miner who had missed 87 shifts in six months, was told that he was better off than the troops in Holland and was then jailed for two months.

Typical wages were hewers 7/- (35p) per shift, and boys (17 years) 2/10d (13p) per shift.

Farming

A young Tom Mitchell (3rd from left)

One afternoon, seated on a corn binder at Harrington Parks Farm, a young university graduate Tom Mitchell had a visit from his old tutor, at Newton Rigg, He had come to offer him a job, helping the Agricultural War effort, little did he know that it would lead to him travelling the world, and he never would remount a corn binder again!

Tom was now a District officer with The County War Agricultural Executive Committee (C.W.A.E.C.s) the **'War Ags'**. These committees were usually made up of eight to ten men, including one agricultural trade unionist, and one lady representing the Women's Land Army; there were 500 in the Country.
As a District Officer (DO), his territory stretched from Distington to the Mountains of Borrowdale and across to Bothel. He was now tasked, to document over 1,202 registered agricultural holdings that stretched over the boundaries of 32 civil parishes.

Nationally between 1941 to 1943 these recordings, were described as 'a modern Domesday book' as every farm in England and Wales was visited.

Each farm was walked, and the different types of land, buildings, cart roads, and soil types delineated on a plan, the farmer was also discreetly graded 'A,''B', or 'C' and note taken of livestock and the types of machinery available, (If any, as there were 649,00 horses on farms in '39.)

Meetings were then held during the day in local halls, schools, and inns later, each farmer would be given an instruction (called the Defence of the Realm Regulation, 18B), which explained the total of extra acres of land he had to plough, and the amount of potatoes or crops to be planted. Also any drainage work to be done, the labour being directed by the Drainage Officer in consultation with the DO.

There was also help in new farming methods i.e., pH of the soil, silage making, dressing with lime and basic slag, the rationing of feeding stuffs, and the licensing of tractors and farm machinery (the Government had placed an advance contract with Ford's); any recalcitrant, had a second meeting with the DO.

One such place for 'War Ags' meeting was the Kirkstile Inn at Loweswater. This eventually developed into the Loweswater Agricultural Society formed in 1940 and still going today.

However being in a 'Reserved' occupation irked Tom, so he enlisted in the RAF for flying duties, but fate took a hand again. While awaiting posting in Canada for advanced flying duties, there was found to be a surplus of pilots for the aircraft available. As the 'War Ags' were listed as the fourth line of Defence, he was duly returned to his duties, in West Cumberland.

The Government's plan was to have two million extra acres under the plough. This was achieved in April 1940, despite the freezing weather throughout January and February. With a further two million in 1940-41, another one and a half million in 1941-42, and in 1942-3 the farmers put in maximum effort, achieving a record crop in the glorious summer of 1943, a feat that the official government historian said **'was magnificent.'**

Farmers with livestock were at a disadvantage, and returns had to be made to qualify for the subsidies attached to grazing on hill land. They were told in the Spring of 1942, that one acre of arable crops fed far more human beings than one acre of grassland, whilst one acre of wheat saved "as much shipping space as seven acres of the best grassland in England."

This extra planting and the shortage of food brought on a virtual epidemic of crop stealing near to towns and villages, though very little was reported in Cumberland.

In addition local farmland was required for training of Troops, Lilly Hall, Winscales, Hunday Farm, Moorhouse Farm and Low Scaw Farm all had to spare some land. However Mr. Furness from Low Scaw farm wrote to his landlady Mrs. Chance, that if she wanted "Owt for t'rent" on that piece of land, she should ask the Military for it. Relations with the military were generally cordial, so much so, that farmers were often called the **'eyes and ears'** of the local defence troops.

Rationing

Begun on the 8th January 1940, five months after the War had started, even though ration books had been issued in 1939 seemed a popular measure inasmuch as hardships would be borne equally by each individual.

The man chosen to be the Minister of Food was Lord Woolton, the head of the Leeds firm of John Lewis. He was aware of the power of good publicity and used wireless programmes, films, articles, posters and meetings to good effect.

He promoted the humble potato and its consumption went up by 60%. Then he let rumours circulate that night fighter pilots were eating lot's of carrots, which enabled them to see in the dark; the consumption of carrots by the nation thereon dramatically increased.

The time table of rationing was:

1940. Rationing by weight, Butter 4ozs, Sugar 12 ozs, Bacon or Ham 4ozs, and £1.0.10d of meat per person, per week.

1940. July. Tea rationed to 2ozs per week, also margarine, cooking fats and cheese, by the same amount.

1941. August. Groups of workers, miners, agricultural workers and fishermen had their allowance increased. Biscuits were now on ration.

1941. Clothes now rationed, 66 coupons per person per year, and was worked out according to the needs of a worker on £3 per week.

A man's overcoat was 16 coupons, and a ladies suit 18; with regulations to the number of pockets, width of trousers and the banning of 'turn ups.' Also the length of men's shirt tails were reduced by two inches.

1941. December. Now a points system (20 a month) introduced for food that had become almost unobtainable: tinned meat, condensed milk, pears or peaches, and a milk allowance of two and a half pints per week, also 1 egg per fortnight.

Distribution of fish now 'controlled.'

1942. Furniture, a range of 22 essential items, buyers having the choice of two qualities and three designs. Range called 'Utility.' Soap allowance 1 lb. per month. Chocolate and sweets on points; 8 ozs per month.

1942. Feb. National Wheatmeal Bread, not rationed, but more of the whole wheat used, resulting in a grey loaf. Healthy but unpopular.

This period of austerity brought a general shabbiness to the nation. The slogan 'make do and mend' applied to clothing, and the favourite slogan 'you've had it' was used when there was nothing left, after enduring hours spent in one of the infamous queues.

Of course there were ways around the shortages, such as the **'Grey Market'**. If a shopkeeper had an excess of food it would be offered to one of his best customers, not the general public, at an inflated price. There was no danger that one of the 900 Food Inspectors who posed as shoppers, found out about the transaction.

Then there was the **'Black Market'** and wholesale profiteering, where £5 would buy a ration book. Tins of peas that cost 5pence at the factory were sold on at 1/2d after being through five hands. Some dealers in the black market tended to dress in a flashy manner, two-tone shoes, hand made suits with wide trilby hats, and given the name 'spivs.'

In Workington, the company secretary of a large provision merchant was fined £500 and sent to prison for two months. He had supplied James Walker of Peterhead, with bacon, ham, lard and three stones of sugar. Unfortunately for them Walker's car had been stopped by the police at Risehow, and he could not account for the goods in his possession.

Women's Land Army

The only women's civilian service under direct government control. Its director and 30 civil servants worked from Balcome Park in Sussex. Over 4,000 were trained, 2,000 were in regular employment, and a further 1,100 under training in farm Institutes, (1940).

About fifty girls were stationed at Bridekirk and Wigton, all directed by the 'War Ags' to farms that needed help, either on a regular or a "one off" basis, where they took their instructions from the farmer, (so long as it had to do with food production). The pay was 48 shillings per week, with one week's leave per year.

The uniform of green jerseys, brown breeches, brown felt slouch hat, and khaki overcoat was often regarded as slightly eccentric, however many discarded it for overalls when threshing or milking on local farms.

The WLA had been reformed in June 39, and up to 1941 approx. 30,000 had volunteered, but this was not enough, many were conscripted. They were

Local WLA. Full Uniform.

mobile and had to work wherever they were sent. There was no standard of discipline, only dismissal, which at times could lead to the auxiliary forces, or other war work.

Local Land Army Girls.

One of their songs called 'Plough Up' began;

> Back to the land, with its clay and sand,
> Its granite and gravel and grit,
> You grow barley and wheat
> And potatoes to eat
> To make sure that the nation keeps fit…

Other jobs undertaken by the **WLA**, were 6,000 in the 'Timber Corps' felling trees, working in saw mills, or selecting trees for poles or timber. Over 20,000 girls were employed as rat-catchers, two girls in Linconshire disposed of 12,000 rats, in one year.

Prisoners of War (POW)

In July 1943 there was over 40,000 Italian prisoners of war at work in the nation's fields; Cumberland was no exception. The camp at Moota (complete with two magnificently decorated chapels) providing well over 100 prisoners (Italian and German) to local farms, some 20% actually coming from farming stock.

The more amenable ones would often live in, but some were not above some simple acts of sabotage, especially German soldiers from the **'Africa Corps'** who when laying drain tiles, would turn a tile at right angles, and cover it up quickly. This was one trick that the district 'War Ags' drainage officers overcame by inspecting the tile runs, before the trench was filled in.

School Children

Also helped the war effort, rose hips were gathered and taken to school to be weighed, before payment, others collected scrap. An official document of the time asked for the collection of rubber, woollens, paper, bones (making glycerine for explosives), and scrap metals. The famous pans (aluminum for Spitfires) being mentioned, and it is noted that an old steel saucepan, would make a rifle bayonet, an old grate would have enough metal to make a Bren gun, and waste paper from a cereal packet was sufficient to make a target. Smaller children attended the Wartime Nursery at Casson Rd, which had provision for 40 children up to the age of five years.

Evacuees

Workington was designated a 'Reception Area' so the Medical Officer of Health asked for 81 ' Lady volunteers' to carry out a house-to-house survey in the districts, to find billets for the intended evacuees.

On the 1st September 1939 a party of 450 children and teachers from Newcastle and South Shields arrived at Workington Main Station, where they were led to St. Michael's school rooms, documented and recorded, then sent to other schools in the Town, also Harrington, Northside, and Siddick.

They were then allocated to local people for their billets. Eventually 1,200 school children and teachers arrived, followed by another 1,250 comprising of adults with children under school age. Evacuees continued to come and go for the duration of wartime, people from Barrow avoiding the bombing, then Londoners fleeing the 'Blitz', and later the Dutch who had a hard winter in 1945. Finally some Jewish children who had survived the camps, arrived after 1945.

Working Life

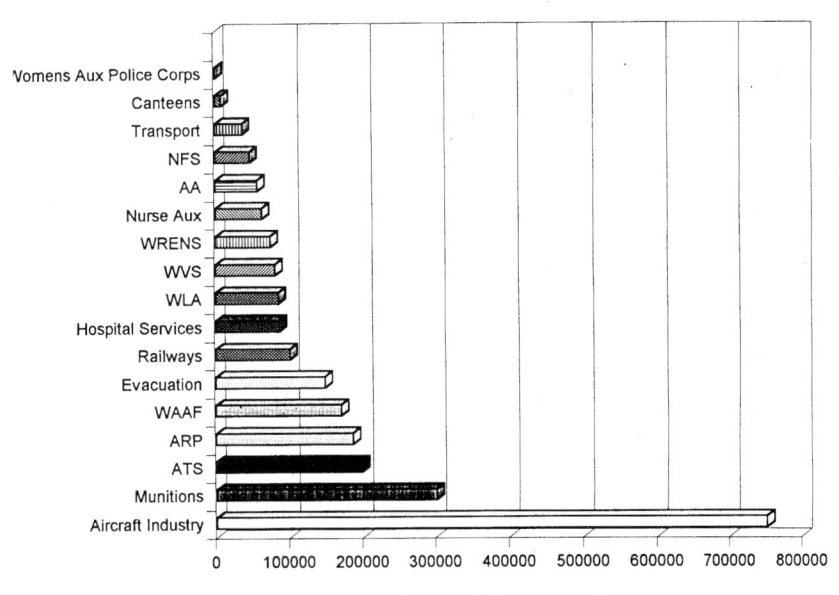

Women's Work in War Time

Civilian Working Life changed. In West Cumberland over 3,400 worked in Royal Ordnance Factories, 2,000 in shell factories and 1,800 employed in aircraft maintenance alone.

These new places of work brought changes, -**Works canteens-** that had been scarce before the war, now provided workers with a bright, clean environment for their meals. Prices in the Ministry of Supply canteens were breakfast 1/-, lunch-1/2d, suppers 1/- and a spam sandwich for 7d.

The new idea of **"Skilled Woman Workers"**, proved a success, as nationally, by 1942, 9 out of every 10 women under the age of 51, were in the forces or industry.

German women were not mobilised until 1944. Britain's women, in the meantime, had allowed thousands of men from industry to be released for active service. They now earned good money. Some factories worked three shifts, with enhanced payment for night-time, and skills were now available to women. They trained as welders, machinists, electricians and mechanics. A degree of independence from the traditional Cumberland jobs of "In service", cleaning or looking after family was noted.

The New Factories

Thermal Syndicate Factory. At Northside, built by J. Leslie and Sons at a cost of £20,000. It made high grade silica quartz glass for valves used in Radar sets for the RAF. Mr G. Lyle managed the young workforce of 92, mainly girls. This factory used massive amounts of electricity and gas, for its arc furnaces. The entire works steel structure, was bonded together with copper straps, being effectively 'degaussed.' A twin factory operated at Wallsend.

Erie Power Hammer HDA.

High Duty Alloys - Distington. A large camouflaged '**SHADOW**' factory Army Ref.-VP477. Built by John Laing and Co. of Carlisle for the new Ministry of Aircraft Production, headed by Lord Beaverbrook.

The site was recommended by John Jackson Adams (later Baron Adams of Ennerdale), to HDA founder Col. Wallace C. Devereux and his advisers. It contained Lilly Hall Farm and the remains of the defunct Distington Iron Works. With a development cost, greater than £1 million and spread over 50 acres, the works alone covered 532,300 sq. feet and later, had one of the largest drop forges (a 20 Ton - American Erie) in the world, which needed to be placed on an intricately designed 3000 ton concrete foundation, forty-eight feet thick.

HDA came to Distington because it was relatively safe from air attack, there was plenty of labour, it had a good supply of water and over 30 feet of blue clay. This acted as a "shock absorber" for the many forging hammers employed.

While the factory was being built, part of the premises of Myers & Bowman's Garage at Prospect, Distington was used as a tool room, the work force being trained in a building at Wilkinson's Wagon Works Moss Bay, with invaluable help from the Technical College. The first product was a small stamping for the Halifax bomber made in Dec 1940.

HDA- Factory - Camouflaged.

Eventually, the work-force of almost 3,000 men and women worked constantly seven days a week. Distington and the surroundings regularly shook, when the hammers pounded day and night.
Finished aluminium alloy forgings, included crankcases, cylinder barrels, general components and propellers for Aero engines. Also thousands of tons of cast material plus a wide range of extruded section.
Some high quality alloy was recycled. Gas to power the large furnaces came from the Steelworks coke ovens, through a special pipe line laid across the fields from the Steel Works.

Shell Factory and Foundry (Munitions) at Drybread on the Marsh, machined the shells, steel warheads, and the brass casing of 3.7inch AA shells; then after filling with explosives they were assembled. Some female labour was also used to strip down Aero engines taken from recovered aircraft at the end of the war.

Cumberland Cloth Co. Northside, (Military Cloth) local name the **'Khaki Factory,'** managed by Crowthers of Huddersfield. While the factory was being built the redundant Havelock Rd premises of Cunninghams machine shop was used for training and limited production.

The new factory received large bales of wool brought by road which was put through a scribbling, spinning and weaving process to make Army greatcoat cloth, ATS and WAAF uniform material and later, cloth for demob suits. During wartime, the total amount of cloth produced was over 1,800 miles in length. Many of these factories were built to the pre war 'Northlight' design.

W.I.S.Co-Section three. Produced steel shell forgings that were taken to the Drybread works for machining; also landing craft shells were waterproofed and ammunition boxes reconditioned. A unit assembled **JEEPS** that arrived in packing crates from Canada. Rumour has it that part of the test run was up to the Half way House on Skiddaw, and when completed, they left the town in convoys of 40 vehicles.

One spin-off was that the good timber from the crates (Pine) was available on ration to local joiners, many houses in Workington, still have Canadian pine floor boards!

WW2 Jeep.

Harrington Magnesite Works- Supplies of magnesium from Austria had been cut off, so this factory was built for the Ministry of Aircraft Production and managed by British Periclose Co. Ltd, employing 200 workers and staff.

Harrington 'Magnasite' Works.

It produced lightly burnt or caustic magnesia from calcinated dolomite and sea water. This was sent by rail to Clifton junction Nr, Manchester to be converted to chlorinated magnesium metal. The Harbour was sealed by towing a concrete caisson (complete with sluice gates and pump house) into position, then sinking it in the entrance. This created a large reservoir for the works, as over 65 million tons of sea water was needed for the large settling ponds. Caustic Magnesium was extracted, at the rate of 800 tons per week, but some of it managed to cover most of Harrington and district, but not the Manager's fine 4 bedroom house, on Scaw road!

The magnesium was used in Aero engines, incendiary bombs and pyrotechnics. Many of the incendiaries dropped on Essen and Cologne in the RAF thousand bomber raids were made with material from Harrington and its sister factory at Hartlepool. The factory cost the huge sum of £850,000 but closed when it was found that the Magnesium cost 4/3d (21p) per pound at Harrington, but 1/7d (9p) elsewhere. It was then 'mothballed' and re-opened for the Korean War, finally closing in 1953.

Distington Haematite & Iron Co. Chapel Bank Works. (Later **D.E.C**), purposely misnamed - the only connection with Distington was the large ornate gates that came from Distington Hall.

The factory was built within a year, the first sod being cut by Bill Poultney, and the first two employees were, G.Westnedge and Tyson Hodgson (Clock numbers 1&2 respectively).

It employed over 1,700, some were steelworkers made redundant by the **W.I.S.Co**. These workers underwent training at Samuel Fox's works in Birmingham.

When production started in June 1942, they made special steel in six 20 Ton electric arc furnaces, producing 2,300 tons per week of special steel, some for ball and roller bearings. (Britain's supply had been cut off when Norway was invaded.)

DEC. Bay 4 'Turned Rounds Section'

Some **Stainless Steel** was produced in a 20 ton furnace. However the bulk of the steel was for armour-plating, and armour-piercing shot much of the 6 Pounder anti-tank shot used at El-Alamein being produced by the company. Its diversity into chrome vanadium steels for gun muzzle brakes, was very successful.

A small unit also fitted flails made from special steel, to mine busting tanks. Another unit was staffed entirely by women burners who cut up local scrap, which was then fed into the electric furnaces.

It was also responsible for operating the town's air-raid siren, and this had to be near a telephone available 24 hours a day. The Management also looked after seven other factories for the MOS.

Wartime Fund-raising

West Cumberland Times and Star. Supported the Troops by organizing the 'Tommy's Smokes Fund.'

Administered by the Chairman Mr. Richardson, Treasurer Lt. Col GT Weir, and Secretary Mr. T. Curry, 400,000 cigarettes had been sent to them by 1941 as well as parcels and smokes for prisoners of war. Some indication of the funds raised, may be calculated, against the price of 200 Wild Woodbines for 4/-. By the time VE day arrived 1,000,000 cigarettes had been sent, along with tobacco, playing cards and pipes. These were used in the prison camps as barter for food from the guards. These supplies continued being sent to troops and prisoners of war up to VE day; however it did not stop. Sid Ogilvie, the secretary, said in '45 "Our work is not finished; many Cumbrians are now fighting the Japs."

Workington's Spitfire Fund

In July 1940 the Mayor Councillor S. Walker was approached by a deputation from the 'Star' Tommies' Smokes Fund with the suggestion that an aeroplane be purchased and be presented to the government. It was unanimously decided that authority be given to the committee to proceed with the scheme.

The first subscription was received from a number of girls from the 'Marsh' who had held a procession and raised 3/6d. By the end of March 1941 £5,000 had been collected and a handing-over ceremony took place in the Opera House on Sunday April 6th 1941.

A cheque for £5,043-16-10d was given to Wing Commander JW Mitchell by 77 year old Mrs Williamson of Harrington, who had chosen a silver bowl as a memento of the occasion.

Ten months passed before the Town heard about its plane - now a Hawker Hurricane 2c BE515 which carried the Borough Coat of Arms & the name Workington. Soon after being attached to a number of UK stations it travelled far, eventually arriving in India on 18th April 1942 and, within a week during a test flight from Drigh Road, it was written off when it crashed into the Malir River on 23rd April 1942.

This successful effort was followed by other National collections,

> Bomber Plane Appeal 1940.
> War Weapons Week in 1941.
> Warship Weeks in 1942.
> Wings for Victory Weeks in 1943.
> Salute the Soldier Weeks in 1944.

Not only did the locals raise money for a fighter aircraft, it adopted a submarine **HMS Porpoise,** a mine-layer, in 1943, when over £25,000 was raised during Warship week. In the advertising campaign, the Trustee Savings bank had drawn on the Nelson legend for its newspaper advert which included this ditty:-

> "Heart of oak are our Ships,
> Jolly tars are our men;
> We always are ready, steady, boys, steady;
> We'll fight and we'll conquer again and again."

This Submarine was built by Vickers at Barrow and launched in 1932 and captained for a time by Commander LW Bennington DSO, DSC, it took part in the Norwegian Campaign and was then based at Malta. Later, in 1945, she failed to return from a mine laying expedition near Penang in the Far East and was the last British submarine to be lost in the war. Two local men served on it at various times, Leading Seaman David Coles, and Steward Arthur Brockbank, the latter one of the 75 crew 'missing' off Penang.

The 1943, Wings for Victory appeal brought in £280,573 from which 10 Mosquito Bombers were purchased. A novel way of collecting funds was adopted by Browne's store on Murray Rd. There, a 1,000 lb. bomb, (empty) had over £76 worth of savings stamps stuck to it. Later it was filled with explosives and 'posted' to Germany - minus the stamps!

The **Workington Times & Star** drew to the attention of its readers that some of the Lake District's Hotels were full of "**Good time Girls**" who were escaping the war. They had cars, lots of petrol, and attended cocktail and bridge parties that were 'in full swing'. The paper urged these '**Slackers in Slacks**' to help the war effort, and started a winter slogan which urged them to, 'Go to it-or Get Out.'
It was calculated that two million people had privately evacuated themselves to Wales, Devon, Scotland, and other quiet areas such as the Lakes. Also that over five thousand people left Southampton for America in the first forty-eight hours after War had been declared.
Newspapers contained numerous adverts for country hotels, and many women passed the whole six years of the War, staying in the comfort of such places, in what the locals called 'funkholes'.
Some of the reporting however, was heavily censored; the standard headline usually began "A Northwest Town" then reported the damage or occurrence many days later, as the Luftwaffe could have obtained information on the effectiveness of its bombing by such accurate reporting.

The **WT&S** still provided interesting reading, there was a regular column about what was happening in Hollywood, written by a local man, David Thursby from Cockermouth. He was an actor based in the USA and had appeared in "Mutiny on the Bounty", "San Francisco", "Captains Courageous", "Sea Hawk", "Mrs Miniver" and "Northwest Passage".

The headlines included such gems, as 'Dance mad girl to join Convent' and 'Cumbrian Women Never Refuse' (a story about the WVS, and their availability for knitting,) and 'Will Service Women return to the Kitchen?'

Aviation

Air crashes sadly became common-place in the area, as flying had increased at the Anthorn, Carlisle, Crosby-on-Eden, Kirkbride and Millom aerodromes. In 1941 a Lockheed Hudson crashed at Loweswater, killing the pilot. Then in 1944 a Vickers Wellington Bomber crashed in the sea off Workington, all the crew were saved by an Air Sea Rescue launch, except the navigator who was drowned.

Youths

Youths (Teenagers had not been invented). After January 1941, they joined the Army or Air Cadets. These organisations aimed to give pre-service training to the youth of the County. Workington Town Boys were in one **Army Cadet Unit**, under Mr. JL Locking, and the St. Benedict Boys Club under Mr. JA Hill in the other. Later a third group assisted by Major E.G Sarsfield-Hall, was formed. All three units were then brought together to form three platoons of a Workington Company.
Mr. H. J. Hobbs became Cadet Captain OC. Cadets, No 1 platoon Commander, Cadet Lt. J.B Fitzpatrick, No 2 Platoon, Cadet Lt. J.A Hill, and No 3 Platoon Lt. H. Stockton With a grand total of over 90 in the Army Cadets alone, all wore the regimental badge of the Border Regiment, and an arm flash consisting of a dragon.

Cadets aimed for the War Certificate "A" that usually took two years, and included tests in sprinting, walking, jumping, vaulting, rope-climbing and swimming. After this, passes in technical subjects were expected. It was much valued, as a job reference, and an introduction to the armed forces.
Various summer camps were attended, the most successful one being in 1942 when over 30 Cadets spent a week under canvas at Bassenthwaite, during which time they were taken up and down mountain sides in jeeps, carriers, and armoured cars by the Army's Driver & Maintenance School (D&M) Keswick.

The **Air Training Corps** (ATC), under the command of Flight Lieutenant Tom Payne, paraded at Guard St. School twice a week. Flight Sergeant Ronnie Leathers was the first member of **1266 Squadron ATC**, to become an RAF pilot, and later flew, the Steelworks Plane after the war. Summer camps were held at Crosby, Longtown, and Millom Aerodromes.

Some Teenagers were in the **Civil Defence Messenger Service**, and attended a Summer Camp held at the Branthwaite Scout Camp. It was noted by the Town Council that it cost 25 Shillings/ £1.25p (Exclusive of third-class travel) per week, for each boy to be trained.

Despite the austere times, boys remained boys. It was all very exciting for some, and one who was acting as an ARP casualty was told to lie on a grassy bank and look very ill. Around his neck was a label stating 'Serious Internal Bleeding'; however after two hours he still had not been found. So, borrowing a pencil he wrote "Bled ta deeth two hoors sen, gon yam."

Some, however, became undisciplined while fathers were away, and more mothers were working. Teachers had been called up, and schools were operating a shift system to cope with the influx of hundreds of extra pupils.

One group appearing in court on the 5th March 1941 before Alderman Mr. F. W. Iredale. Five boys, aged between 10 & 13, were charged with breaking and entering. Retribution was swift, all the children were 'birched,' the thirteen year old ringleader had been interviewed 119 times by the Probation Officer, so he received four strokes.

Guides
There was one Ranger Company, seven Companies of guides and seven Brownie packs. Summer camps were held at Lamplugh attended by the District Commissioner, Mrs Wilson Young.

Leisure Activities
There appeared to be a very acceptable and varied social life available to the towns' folk during WW2.

Cinemas in Workington were **The Ritz**, new and up-to-date, complete with Thomas Hudson on the mighty Wurlitzur organ.

On 8th April 1940, *'The Stars look Down'* was shown, a dramatic masterpiece reflecting life in a coal mine, starring Michael Redgrave, Margaret Lockwood and Emlyn Williams, Director Carol Read.

This picture was shot chiefly on location in West Cumberland (as was the Workington Story) with local school children in exterior scenes. The Ritz management called 'come and see yourselves on film'- many did, with Michael Redgrave addressing the audience on opening night.

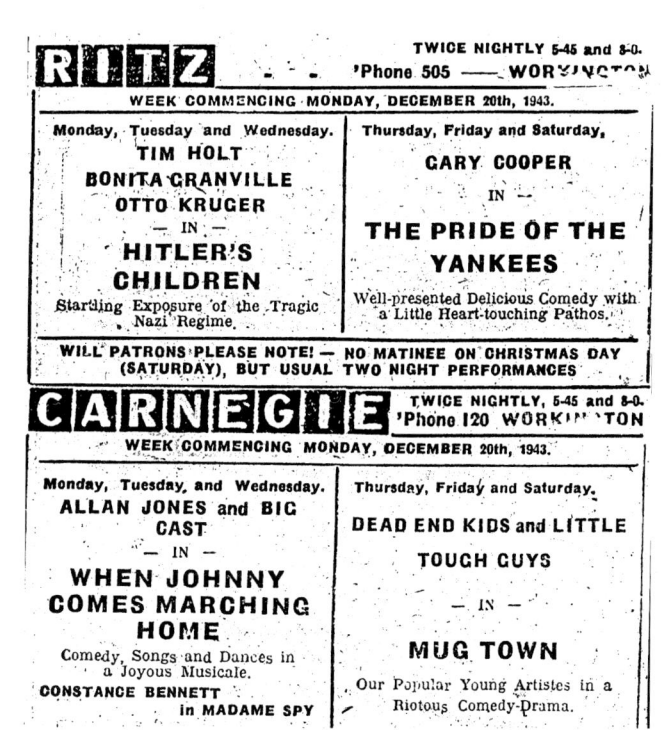

Cinema Advert 1943.

The Oxford, cinema in Oxford Street, showed *'Vogues of 1938'* (a gay musical) and the **Hippodrome** on Hagg Hill featured Jack Holt in *'Trapped by the G. Men.'*

Here the queue for the first house on a rather cold February night was assailed by a speaker Mr Peter Grice, one of Sir Oswald Mosleys, 'Blackshirts,' perched on the back of a car. He and Mr Watson Bowie from the British Union of Fascists, urged the cinema-goer's to join them. After twenty minutes they gave up, and drove back to Carlisle. For Mosley, the fascist leader, (who had been one of the most able of the

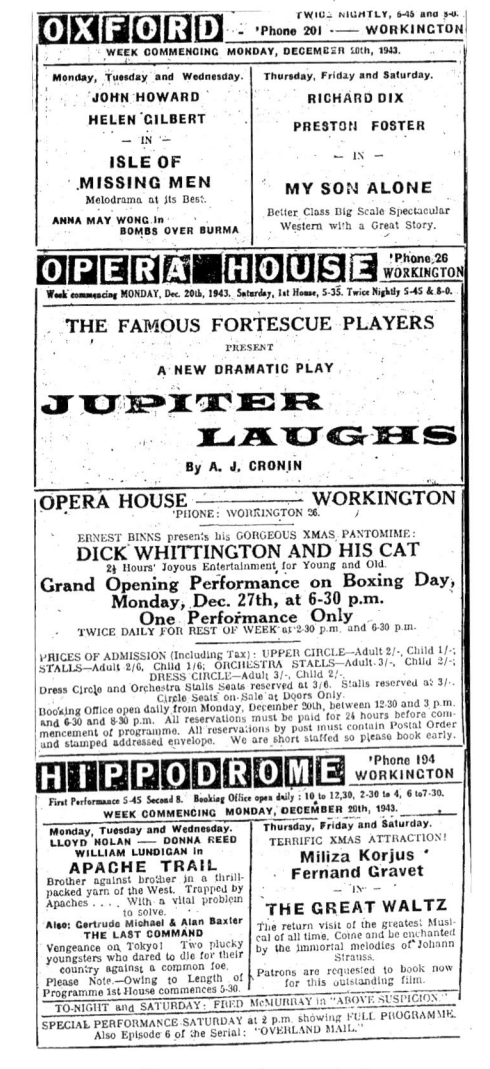

Opera House Advert 1944.

Cinema Advert 1943.

politicians,) was imprisoned along with his accomplices, but was released due to ill health, and into virtual house arrest in 1943.

At the **Carnegie** there were two houses of *'Love under Fire'* starring Lorreta Young and Don Ameche.

The **Opera House** was the premier venue for live shows, such as *'Wigan and proud of it'* a revue by Tom Moss, followed a few days later, by Miss Nora Grunn and Anne Ziegler singing 'Toubers - Birds in the Forest.'

An all together different brand of singing could be heard in the 'Crooning Competition' at Workington's **Albert Hall**, the winner being decided by audience applause, admission 6d (5p).

The **Hippodrome Ballroom** was held a 'Short night Dance - 7 to 11pm, and during the summer a Carnival Ball was organised by the 5th Battalion Border Regiment HG, in the Drill Hall.

Lonsdale Park Stadium staged greyhound racing on Mon/Wed/Fri, at 7:15pm admission 1/- (5p).

Meanwhile **Workington Reds**, football club were playing Mansfield at Borough Park, loosing 1-Nil.

Workington Bright Sparks Social Club. Formed in 1939 by a group of young people who regularly met on Murray Rd. At the first meeting in Archers Café, they elected the Mayor, Councillor WA Palmer as their President, Mr CA Stephenson the Chairman, Mr Alan H. Sandwith, Vice Chairman, Mr ST Dodds secretary and Mr David Hill treasurer.
Committee, comprised, the Misses, M. Legros, R. Fletcher, M. Hyde and Vera Grim-Zevitch, with Messrs F. Doggart, J. Caruthers, K. Byers and H. Anderson.

Their aims were to raise funds for war time charities-cigarettes for local soldiers, Red Cross and other organisations, and to brighten up the 'blackout'.

Their first fund raising dance was in St Michael's Parish rooms, on 9th November 1939, dancing to the 'Selma' Band. More than sixty young people indulged in games ranging from 'Winkie' to the 'Noble Duke of York,' statue dancing, and musical knees.

The Mayor. WA Palmer.

From this core, emerged a dynamic social group that held games, competitions, dances, discussions, cinema shows, and sing-songs also walking, boating and cycling trips.
A concert party was quickly formed under the name of 'Flashes from the Bright Sparks'. This was so successful that it toured the county, giving shows to the RAF at Silloth, Soldiers and ATS at Carlisle Castle, and filled local village halls for months.
Funds were needed for Workington Infirmary so they put on a Celebrity Concert by the BBC & London Concert Artists, with Lorery Dyer, Soprano, Robert Easton, Bass Baritone, and the United Steel Companies Orchestra, conductor Millie Booth.
When this group eventually disbanded, they had exceeded all their fund-raising targets, many of their members became prominent in the business and the social life of the town.

Culture was to be found at the **WEA** at St Johns parish rooms, while at the **Tech College** a learned talk on 'Economic Geography' was given.

A rendering of 'Professor Tim' was staged by Our Lady and St Michael's Players in St Joseph's school hall.

Maryport

Bomb blast damage to 1 Ingleby Terrace, Camp Road, Maryport.

The second world war brought a brief period of increased trade and a drop in unemployment to the town, however most activity was centred on the port and the new factory estate.

The Docks

Named the Elizabeth and Senhouse Docks, up to 1944 had handled 1,297 ships, importing only 6,300 tons. Contrasting with over 530,824 tons exported, mainly 'coals from Newcastle' and the North East. Over half was shipped to Northern Ireland, fuelling the war industry, with the rest going to Southampton, Plymouth and London. A coal chute that was capable of loading 250 tons per hour was in use 24 hours a day, and the local labour force responded magnificently, and unlike Workington, there were neither stoppages nor strikes during the entire hostilities.

The RAF had offices on the South quay, as the bombing targets for the Solway range were refurbished, and towed onto site, ready for the air gunners to practise on.

The heavy engineering firm of Drummonds, based at Workington, fitted prefabricated gun mountings, ready use ammunition lockers and degaussing cables to a considerable number of merchant ships in the port, which was considered safe from attack.

The town's lifeboat saved the four crew members of the 'Mourne Lass,' a herring drifter that was sinking two and a half mile out in the Solway. For this brave and gallant act, the coxswain was awarded the RNLI bronze medal.

Defences

There were many road blocks around the town, their purpose was to slow down any invading forces, and secondly to stop and search civilian vehicles for security and any black market dealing. These roadblocks usually consisted of cylinders filled with concrete, and a narrow entrance that could be closed by steel rails. Some strange ones were employed. The County Council had at least two outside the town in which

An Alan Williams Turret Pillbox

coils of barbed wire sprang out of the road when the large cast iron covers were removed.

These road blocks were situated at Camp End Ellengrove, on the Cockermouth road, across the Prom, at the Station Hotel Grasslot, and on the Ellenborough Old Road. Besides these defences there were pill boxes, one on the pier, and a rare machine-gun turret, made of steel, called an 'Allan Williams Turret pillbox.' On the 'brows' a AA unit with a 4 inch gun, later 1x75mm of the 561 Coast Regiment, had taken up a commanding position.

Both the north and south coastlines of Maryport were extensively mined; these caused problems after fierce storms hit the area, in 1943. Some of these large mines had been washed out of place and onto the beach. A company of **Royal Engineers** hurriedly detonated the ones that were in danger of being taken out to sea.

The first mine detonated caused extensive damage to Flimby school, the master's house, 5 Criffel Rd and the police house. There was also widespread damage to Fothergill and Risehow. There were no casualties as the villagers had been evacuated for the day. Later, another mine at Bank end, again under controlled detonation, damaged Maryport cemetery, "Sea View" Cross Cannonby, Crosby and Birkby.

On the night of 21st July 1940, an air raid by a German Dornier 217 bomber, left seven people dead, five wounded and the British School destroyed.

Three local men took advantage of one air raid alert, and burgled the Athenian warehouse; their loot was enormous. Not only did they steal boots, shoes and clothing in large amounts, but the ever popular cigarettes, 7,100 of them. All three were arrested and later jailed.

During Warship week, the war savings' committee asked the townsfolk to buy bonds and savings certificates. This resulted in the grand sum of £362,000 being raised, enabling the trawler/mine sweeper **HMS Mangrove** to be adopted. In war weapons week £72,000 was raised, and later, in "Wings for Victory Week" £70,000 Mr Aston, the war savings assistant commissioner from Carlisle, said that the town should buy a squadron of Spitfires, this resolution was moved by Miss SS Donaldson and seconded by Reverend AL Web.

Many other collections took place for wartime funds tended to run out rather fast. In 1943 there was a Red Cross penny a week appeal, the Vicar of Maryport Rev Derek Gordon Blake spearheaded the fund, aided by the chairman, Mrs Denwood and the treasurer, Mr GNS Porter. The Red local Cross funds were swelled by £1,626.

In 1943 a new British restaurant opened in Senhouse St. It was formally opened by Mr F. Mulgrew, the Council Chairman, who said that 'this development was proof, that the council, had vision.'

In February there had been 2,792 servings of soup, 4,654 servings of 'meat and two veg' and 5,453 puddings had been eaten, along with 1,657 cups of tea. However, there was a price increase on its way, 'meat and two veg' was to be increased from seven to eight pence.

A local communist, John Rafferty, also set up a wartime exchange and mart in the town.

Solway Estate New Factories

This was the first purpose-built estate for the new West Cumberland Industrial Development Company Ltd. It covered 26 acres, and was designed to lower the male unemployment situation that was at 78%. Among the firms using the estate were:

E G Pierce & Co. (London.) Manufacturers of surgical instruments and hypodermic needles; up to 1939 most surgical instruments were imported from Germany. This new factory produced instruments from stainless steel and employed over 50 people.

British Bata Shoe Co. Ltd. The Chairman Maj. Gen. E. L. Spears (MP for Carlisle) encouraged the factory to settle in Maryport. The first leather shoes were produced in March 1941, by some of the 200 workers who had been trained at the main factory in Tilbury. The initial batch of sandals went to the West Indies. Then after building a new extension and recruiting 200 more employees, they then produced footwear (wellington boots & canvas shoes) for the Ministry of Supply (MOS).

Lakeland Food Industries. The owners fled Hitler's regime and arrived from Czechoslovakia.

The factory became a preserve centre in 1939 and employed 220 people canning and bottling all English fruits, strawberries, peas, meat and picnic tongues. The imported Commonwealth goods preserved were tomato sauce, and fruit such as pears, apricots and pineapples. This factory was the first to can fruit salad, and was known locally as the 'Jam Factory'.

Hornflowa. Millions of buttons for the armed forces were produced by this factory. Another European émigré Dr Hertzberg, started the button-making process at

Maryport; this entailed grinding down the hooves & horns of animals to a powder in four stages.
It was then mixed with a fixer under heat & pressure. The buttons were formed, drilled, painted khaki then polished and shipped out by road. It was calculated that the turnover of the firm was about £1.2 million at today's prices.

Entertainment. The cinema was still the place to try and evade the wartime blues however during some weeks this could not be avoided, as the CARLTON was showing *'Stick to your Guns'* followed by *'Burma Convoy'*. In a contrast the EMPIRE provided *'Love Crazy'*(an original comedy) followed by *'Smiling Through'*(romance with delightful singing).

In the Baptist hall, Miss W. Richardson BSc. from the Cumberland and Westmorland farm school at Newton Rigg, was giving a down-to-earth lecture on 'Fertilisers and Manure'(a better way to grow Winter greens).After a well-debated question and answer session, she was thanked by the Rev HL Duff.

Maryport was close to the airfields that were situated on the Solway plain, and there was a large amount of flying near the town. In May 1943 a mid-air collision between a Avro Anson and a Vickers Wellington scattered wreckage over the Ellenbrough area, tragically all nine on board died, but fortunately none of the townsfolk.
Hurricanes and their pilots came to grief at various times, including one at Mawbray, another at Dovenby, plus one on the Moota Road, to name a few.
At Dearham a Bristol Beaufighter crashed beside the bridge, and a Lockheed Hudson came down on the edge of the village. Many of the pilots and crew were killed. Thankfully, most of the flying was without incident, considering the number of aircraft flying over West Cumberland.

Cockermouth

HQ Unit

On the 20th July, 1940, Colonel GJ Pocklington-Senhouse, T. D, assumed command of the 4th Battalion, assisted by, Capt. Bob Starkie, Capt. Bill Farmer, Capt. N. P. Banks, Lt Joe Starkie and Sgt Sid Armstrong the PSI.

Their HQ was in the Drill Hall. The battalion was responsible for six road blocks at strategic points around the town. Eventually, there were four companies, 79 officers, and 1,473 men enlisted.

Weapon practice, with Blacker Bombards, P14 rifles, Sten Guns, BARs, and Pattern 45 grenades, was on the old yeomanry range (the Butts) at the 'Hay' on the Cockermouth to Higham Rd.

Air Raid Precautions came under Mr J. Conkey, Chief warden, assisted by Mr OS Macdonald his deputy. They all used the Bridge St rooms for training purposes.

Hound Trail at Loweswater

Whitehaven

One of the Whitehaven Battery's 138mm M10 guns.

The town was of no military importance, but there were mines and factories nearby; also it was a port. This had to be defended against invasion and kept open for the many sailings of coasters that carried thousands of tons of coal, some transported from the North East to needy areas.

The Coastal Battery

The men of 422 Coast Battery, 561 Coast Regiment were billeted on the 'Brows' Bransty, with their guns. The Battery consisted of 2x4" BL MKVII Naval Guns, of French origin, and two Lewis Machine Guns.

The two four inch were soon sent to the DMS service, and two powerful 138mm, M10 Guns off the French Cruiser, Paris, which had been seized in Plymouth in 1940, were placed in the Battery, and operated by men of the Royal Artillery and later, a Home Guard Unit. Two powerful 90cms searchlights with a generator also occupied a fortified bunker, built into the bottom of the cliff,

90cms searchlight-projector

50

the orders being co-ordinated by field telephone.

Vessels approaching Whitehaven Harbour would fly the flag of the day, determined by a retired rear Admiral (and his ADC Captain Maitland-Kirwan RN), stationed at the port. They were then required to 'heave to' in the examination anchorage, covered by the arc of fire of the examination battery. They would then be examined by a small vessel from the port, who would place an armed guard on board if necessary. This could be a risky manoeuvre, as it took place under the watchful eye of the Battery commander, day and night.

Pte Jim McCourt (65) Whitehaven's Oldest Home Guard.

Col IW Burns-Lindow, CO 6th Battalion.

Captain V.H.P. Roberts, RA had occasion to fire a 'Bring to Round' over the bows of an errant vessel, and as to be expected when over five-inches of high explosives passed over the ship, and then detonated, the vessel's captain, his mind now focused, conformed to the order, although the rumours later, about how close it was, rather exaggerated the gunners' skills!

Regular Units were the Royal Artillery (Bransty Battery) and a detachment of Royal Marines billeted on the old quay and operating a 100 foot steel and concrete lookout tower. A battalion of the Auxiliary Pioneer Corps was also on hand at Egremont if required.

6th Battalion Home Guard

Col Burns-Lindow DSO, was the first CO, followed by Lt Col W. McCowan, with Major WG Sumner. Second in Command, and Capt. J. Tyndell Adjutant. The unit was split into platoons the Pit Guard, Dock Platoon, Transport Section, Railway Section, Electricity Section and Platoons at Hensingham and Distington. At one time the battalion owned a Rolls Royce armoured car that they had built themselves from an old taxi.

Recruits find sloping arms a problem

When the 6th Battalion held its first large scale exercise, German paratroops were supposed to have landed at St Bees and then fought their way into the town. The Home Guard put up stiff opposition and captured the lot. However the local populace got in the way. After suffering many ribald comments, the handcuffed 'enemy' soldiers had to be extracted through the jeering crowds from the archway, next to Dixon's fish shop in the Market place.

A strong letter from the CO appeared afterwards in the Whitehaven News, warning the locals about being mixed up in military affairs, and that real Germans, would soon have had them 'shifted'!

But three weeks later, soldiers are quite "at ease"

Local Home Guardsmen with a Lewis Gun.

TA Recruiting Parade Whitehaven.

Recruiting Parade in the Market.

SS. Herbert Walker

Docks

Under the control of Harbourmaster Captain Thompson, it was mostly one way traffic; coal out. Thousands of tons were shipped to Northern Ireland ports - Belfast, Newry, Carrickfergus, Portaferry, Londonderry and Kilkeel, by the local Broker- JG Oldfield.

Approximately one third coal exported from Cumberland came from the Whitehaven pits. Some coal was shipped to Fleetwood, Liverpool and the Isle of Man. Vessels that made regular calls were the *"Karri", "Poplar", "Beconia", "Ben Varry", "Saint Enoch", "Broom", "Manxsona", "Ben Yooar"* and the *"Alpha"*.

However, one of the most welcome was the small Coaster ' SS Herbert W. Walker, for it could carry 330 tons of stores into Whitehaven.Its sister ship, the 'SS Cumbria' carried 240 tons of coal to Irish ports. Both were owned by the Wilson Steam Ship Co. Ltd.
The SS Herbert W. Walker's usual cargoes from Liverpool, included-sugar-26tons/ 12cwts, feeding meal-10 tons, canned goods-34 tons, beans-1 ton, sundries 1 ton, and beer 10ton/ 8cwts! The dock and harbour were out of bounds to the public for a time, and guards were placed at strategic points.
One night a sentry stopped a couple of inebriated Irish travellers who had strayed near the dock gates. "Who goes there" he challenged, back came the oath "Jesus, Mary, Mother of God" to which the sentry replied "advance and be recognised both of you"!

The Harbour

This was invaded, not by the enemy but by the friendly Danes. Two of the first vessels to arrive were the 'Ami' and the sixty feet long *'Brynhild.'* This vessel had been fishing off the dogger bank when the skipper 'Valdemar' and the crew, heard, over the wireless, that Denmark had been invaded. Discussions took place with other boats, and later a broadcast by the British government, said that Danish boats were welcome to sail to British waters for protection, and their crews would be treated as British fishermen. Paul Pedersen was one of the crew, of the 'Olympia' from Esbjerg, and at nineteen, was already an experienced merchant sailor. So his vessel sailed into Grimsby, where he along with many other fishermen, were billeted in a sawmill at Immingham for six weeks.

During this time they were interviewed and allowed time to visit Grimsby. Later, they fished out of this port, but were harassed by German aircraft. They were given machine guns and trained how to use them - the attacks stopped. Then the government decided that the East coast was too dangerous for fishing, as there were loose mines, marauding 'E' boats, and attacks by the Luftwaffe, so the boats were allocated to ports in the north-west.

The fleet was escorted to the Moray Firth by a destroyer, steaming at 8/10 knots, however the 'Brynhild'(with Paul Pedersen) and two other vessels, could only manage 4 knots, so they made their own way unescorted, through the Caledonian canal to Whitehaven, some other boats going to Fleetwood.

At Whitehaven, some of the port's elderly vessels were doing duty as barrage balloon

The MA Kirk. Circa 1989.

anchors at Fleetwood and Liverpool, so the Danish seine netters were provisioned, fuelled, and after being fitted with a Lewis gun on the stern, and undergoing gunnery practice with CPO Simm, went to fish in Icelandic Waters. The trips lasted between 16-21 days depending on the weather, the port of Thorshavn in the Faroes as a provisioning port.

Two other boats sailed in after three months, the 'MA Kirk' skippered by Hans Anderson, and the 'C. Riesager' with Niels Thomson. They were followed in 1942 by the twelve others including the *"Karen Marie"*, *"Fylla"*, *"Gerda"*, *"NV Lydia"* and the *"Vidar"*.

The hazards of fishing were long hours, cold and the sea. The 'C. Riesager' turned "turtle" off the Shetland Isles, and was only saved by the self righting effect of its heavy keel and some water-tight compartments. Over three tons of ropes had to be cut away and the engine repaired before steaming back to port. The only casualty being the cabin boy who had suffered from the effects of hypothermia. He recovered so quickly that he sailed back to Icelandic waters as cook on the *"Amy"* two days later. This vessel was eventually requisitioned by the government, and took part in the D-Day landings.

Then on a trip from the Faroes the *"Brynhild"* struck a mine, which took some heart stopping seconds to explode. Thankfully the boat, by then, was just out-of-range from the effects of the explosion, and was able to continue ten more days of uninterrupted fishing.

The *Lyda* was fishing near to the prohibited southern Irish waters when she came under scrutiny by the periscope of a submarine. Hugo Thinnesen the mate was working at the stern, and saw the circling, U. Boat. He quietly told the skipper, Chris Nelson, about the intruder. Later they steamed back to Whitehaven and had to report the incident to Lt Parish RNVR. When asked why they thought the 'sub' was German, they replied "If it was British then they would have come up for a feed of fish!"
Previously, Norman's the grocers in town, had included some rarely-seen oranges when making up the provisions. Little did he know that they were considered bad luck by the Danes. These, along with whistling, were strictly taboo on board; strong words were spoken on the vessel's return.
The rewards were large, for a good catch, which was mainly flat fish (sole or witches), bulked in the hold (between layers of ice). A complete hold full of fish in peacetime, would be worth £100. Now, during wartime, the same quantity was worth £1700, and guaranteed by the Government. The Danes measured their catches in 'Kits' (1 Kit = 10 stone).

A stone of prime haddock in 1938 cost 4/- (20p), but in 1941 it cost 18/- (90p), the skippers, mates and deck hands were in dangerous, but well-paid jobs.
Most of the catch was bought by the local firm of **TW Dixon**, who sent it to London by rail. It was said many times during the London Blitz, the only fish at Billingsgate was from Whitehaven.

Some fishermen stayed on after wartime and made West Cumberland their home, some went back to Grimsby, but most returned to Denmark after VE day, leaving behind a legacy of good seamanship, and the landing of large catches of fish, in excellent condition. The Danes also had a good friend in the honorary Danish Consul, Mr Singleton, of Prospect House Distington who looked after their affairs.

The Radio Station

Hidden in the Whitehaven Brick and Tile Co. Ltd, Low Road site. (This company had supplied 14 Million bricks in wartime.) The small concrete building was behind the main kilns and contained a single bed, emergency rations, and a first aid kit. Its dipole aerial was suspended between the works twin-chimneys. This station was one of 60, low power (100W) 'H' Stations all transmitting the BBC Home Service (0203.5 metres - medium wave), between the hours of 6.30am and 11pm, (although it was manned for 24 hours a day) the programmes were being piped in By GPO Landlines, from the BBC's bomb proof centre at Bristol.

Typical programmes broadcast in the Home Service, included
- 5pm   Children's Hour
- 6pm   News
-         News in Norwegian
- 6.45   Women in Wartime-The WAFF
- 7.30   Cyril Fletcher
-         Beethoven Concert
-         Variety Programme
- 9pm   News - topics
-         Picture postcard
- 10pm Religious Programme
-         News in Gaelic
-         PG Woodhouse Stories
- 11pm National Anthem & Close down.

These low power stations were designed to stop the enemy locking on to them, as it had been found that the previous high power stations, located in major cities, had aided German aircraft who simply tuned in, and flew towards the increasingly strong signal.

However the station engineer, Mr Jenkins, had another task. If Britain was invaded, newscasts to the local populace and the defence force and auxiliary, units, were to be given by the chief liaison officer, Mr JJ Adams (later Baron Adams) and his deputy, the Manager of the Whitehaven News, Mr JR Williams. Both had distinctive voices and were well known in the area, (these two also had accesses to a secret transmitter kept for an emergency),

During the night, a mysterious voice over the telephone (tested every hour) would ask for the transmitter to be switched on at various strengths and passages of music had to be played- to who, in the middle of the night, the young engineer Mr Ian H McDonald was never told, nor did he know that explosives were on hand, to prevent the station falling into enemy hands.

Another group interested in radio transmissions was the 'shadowy' members of the **RSS (Radio Security Service)** who maintained a radio-listening watch for signals generated locally and from the Continent, including those from British agents. Results of these intercepts were sent through coded messages, to a Post Office Box in Barnet.

The **RSS** members (mainly ex radio hams) were generally given a cover of being in the ROC, as "special observers" and issued with the blue uniform beret and badge. This stopped people asking them awkward questions, about their non-contribution to the war effort. Indeed any inquisitive officials were to be told "we are engaged in secret radio-location work" and given the phone number of the head of RSS, Lieutenant Colonel Maltby.

Another clandestine force was also at large, this was the British resistance organisation who operated under the deliberately vague name of **Auxiliary Troops**. It had been formed by Major Colin McVean-Gubbins under the aegis of GHQ Home Forces. To cover up their activities, they wore Home Guard uniforms with the '202 Battalion Flash'.

The bases were top secret, and tended to be large underground concrete bunkers, well hidden, and capable of sustaining the four-man teams for weeks. These 970 'setts' were well stocked with food, water and the latest weapons, including Thompson sub-machine guns, Mills bombs, sticky bombs, anti-tank mortars, plastic explosives and time pencils.

Over 5,000 men were in this secret army, which was to fight the Germans if invasion took place. Their task was to carry out acts of sabotage and disruption. It was calculated that their life behind enemy lines would be in the order of days not weeks. There is no evidence that the Auxiliary Patrols operated in West Cumberland. However, there may have been some Auxiliary Signals units in the area. When the Local Forests were used again in 1946, a hut with two transmitter/receivers was discovered a sure sign, of an Auxiliary Signals unit.

Auxiliary Patrol Badge.

The Radar Station
Situated alongside St Bees Lighthouse, gave warning of aircraft or shipping movements, and was of the Chain Home Low type. With the station being then high tech and top secret, it was staffed by many RAF and WAAF personnel who, in turn, were guarded by over 50 Infantry men of the Border Regiment.

The buildings to accommodate these personnel, consisted of a 'Reveted' Transmitter and receiver block, generator house (although main's electricity was laid on) a guard house, cook house, barracks, lorry park and an armoury.
Perhaps it was indicative of the different roles they were carrying out. Many of the

RAF were billeted out, in St Bees and Sandwith, whilst the WAAFs stayed at Garlieston, a large house on Corkickle. The Army, for security and defence reasons, had wooden barracks on site; winters spent on the St Bees headland must have left a lasting impression!

A Typical Chain Home Low, Radar Tower.

Air Raid Precautions

This group was also perched on a hill. The men (and after a long struggle, women) of the No2 A & B, **Bransty Branch ARP Post,** operated at the Old Bransty Hospital for 24 hours, per day.

The ARP manual rather curiously stated 'Air raid wardens should be men generally over 30 years of age, or women.' *They should be of good character level-headed and free from obvious physical or temperamental disability. On general grounds the older men and women with a good sense of responsibility and of a type to inspire confidence amongst their neighbours will be most suitable.* It was planned that in urban areas there would be a Wardens post of five or six wardens to every 400 to 500 inhabitants. Each warden should have a thorough knowledge of their sector, of its people, and the location of gas mains, electric cables, telephones, shelters and trenches.

The Bransty post was soon staffed, and throughout the 'phoney' war, carried out exercises and checked the area for breaches of the blackout regulations.

These regulations were aimed to prevent lights being shown to enemy bombers, as they passed over Whitehaven, en-route to Glasgow, and to prevent injury if local bombing did occur. To this end, each householder had public information leaflets and an ARP book. Brown paper was stuck over glass door panels, and windows taped. Thick curtains were placed over windows and doors. A refuge room had to be chosen (usually one with thick walls and small windows). It was then stocked with washing materials, disinfectant, bandages, and food.

However trouble was brewing-**Civil Defence HQ** at 15 Duke St, was dragging its heels in implementing the appointment of 'Housewife' Wardens, and the lasses of Bransty were asking awkward questions.

Trouble flared up from another direction. An urgent request was made for the constable to attend the National School after dark, as couples were using ARP sand bags, as a 'loitering place.' However, the wardens along with members of Rescue and Demolition Parties, were soon busy, attending courses at the Council's Coach Road Depot, on such diverse subjects as Stirrup Pumps, UXB's - (Unexploded Bombs), and Gas Warfare - a notice of which, was pinned on the wall.

The wardens held their last meeting on the 6th of Febuary 1945 and were disbanded. It was revealed that after having a dispersal sale of effects, including the dart board (sold to the British Legion for £2), and the wireless, (given to the work house), a sum of £13 7s 6p was now in the kitty.

ALL GAS

If you get a choking feeling, and a smell of musty hay,
You can bet your bottom dollar that there's phosgene on the way.
But the smell of bleaching powder will inevitably mean
That the enemy you are meeting is the gas we call chlorine.
When your eyes begin twitching, and for tears you cannot see,
It is'nt mother peeling onions, but a dose of C.A.P.
If the smell resembles pear drops, then you'd better not delay,
It's not father sucking toffee, it's that ruddy K.S.K.
If you catch a pungent odour as you are coming home for tea,
You can safely put your shirt on it, they're using B.B.C.
And lastly, while geraniums look pleasant in a bed,
Beware their smell in war-time; if its lewisite, you're dead.

Notice displayed on the wall at Bransty ARP Post.

When a Housewife-Warden proposed that the money be given to charity, the log book stated that a **"heated discussion"** took place She was eventually overruled and everyone had a night out at the Legion, the residue of money being donated to the Hospital Fund!

Stationed in ARP Headquarters was Col. RW Burnyeat divisional controller, Mr J. Gillmour and Col. PDC Johnston DSO, deputy divisional controllers.

The Tower Brewery was used as a storage depot for the Civil Defence, who was also responsible for the new 25hp Armstrong Siddeley Ambulance which cost £850, and could be operated with one man with its mobile stretcher.

Lowca also raised an ARP Post, first at the Lowca Welfare Institute but then transferred to the Colliery, where it had a fire-fighting and first-aid team. Among the people attending the first meeting was Chief ARP Warden, Mr P Dalton, J W Brown, S Curwen, W Hoodless, T Brown, W Dixon, JB Little, H Park, W Vernon, H Collins, J Armstrong, T Denwood, A McLean, and T Crelling.

Police Inspector J Little, Whitehaven

Home Defence

A Handley Page 42E Horsa.

Royal Observer Corps
It seemed that every hill around Whitehaven was given over to defence, and the land at Harras Moor was no exception, the volunteers of the **ROC** being based there.

This post that was one of the first in the area worked in conjunction with others at Eskdale, Millom and Seascale, all reporting to the Lancaster, 29 Group RAF.

The sites had common equipment, ie, 'the post instrument' with a Micklethwaite height correction attachment, mounted on a circular, gridded map of the area, a telephone link with RAF District Command and flares to warn off any stricken - friendly aircraft which were in danger of colliding with high ground.

The Whitehaven post got one over on Workington, as General Eisenhower's aircraft was being tracked from the Ayrshire coast. It flew above the cloud and could not be seen by the Workington ROC observers, only to be picked up by the Whitehaven observers, when it became visible above Harras Moor.
On the 27th June 1941 they were harassed by a drifting **Barrage Balloon** that had broken from its moorings, uprooting electricity poles and transformers causing hundreds of pounds worth of damage in the Harras Moor-Aikbank Farm Area.

Aviation
The increase in air activity over West Cumberland brought danger. Hostile enemy aircraft which flew mainly at night were looking for targets, especially when they returned from their blitz on Glasgow and Clydebank, and dropped their surplus bombs, guided by any stray chinks of light.

Workington, Maryport, Barrow and Sellafield all suffered from bombing. One Luftwaffe bomber pilot nearly scored the biggest hit of his life! His discharged bombs dropped in a field alongside Low Sellafield Farm, the only damage being to some stained glass windows. However if it had landed on the other side of the farm, the giant Sellafield ROF Factory would have exploded along with hundreds of tons of TNT within the site.

Our planes also gave cause for alarm. On August the 7 1940 at 1:30 in the afternoon, farmer Matthew Dickinson, and his staff, of West Croft Farm Pica were having their lunch. A shadow fell over the farm house, followed by a loud bang. One of the strangest aeroplanes had crash-landed. It was a twin wing Handley Page 42E, named 'Horsa,' the military version of the Hannibal Class, originally used by Imperial Airways for carrying 38 passengers, over distances up to six hundred miles.

Only three of the original eight, were still flying. It was a huge aircraft, 90 feet long with a wing span of almost 130ft, powered by four Bristol-Jupiter engines, each capable of producing 490 hp.
The crew, captained by Pilot Officer EG Libbey was safe. The aircraft with 271 Squadron was elderly, and carrying 3000lbs of ammunition from Manchester-Ringway to Stornaway. It had caught fire, in mid-air, and had to make a hurried emergency landing, fortunately without injury to the five airmen on board.
No sooner had he and his crew reached the farmhouse, when a platoon of soldiers arrived, during which time the plane blew up, causing all concerned to take cover, the live ammunition going off in all directions, and must have given the soldiers a taste of battle conditions, on the remote Cumbrian moor.

Then on the 14th October 1943, Whitehaven had a 'near miss' when an Avro Anson broke up in mid air over the Kells/Thwaiteville area. There were no civilian casualities but the crew of five were killed. Some, possibly having tried to bail out at low level, were found wrapped up in their parachutes.
By coincidence, a Battle of Britain fighter pilot Flt. Lieut. David Moor Cook had been presenting the town with a commemorative 'Wings for Victory' Plaque at the Gaiety cinema, and was having tea with the Manager of the Whitehaven News, Mr JR Williams. They both went to the scene of the crash and the pilot took away some vital instruments, but was heard to say "what a tragic waste of life."

Cadet Corporal Leonard Wells BEM and his Parents

A very brave rescue of a Pilot, Sgt Buckee from a crashed and blazing, two seat Miles Martinet at Seascale, on the 2nd May 1944, earned a 20 year old Egremont ATC Cadet Corporal Leonard Wells, the British Empire Medal, presented by the King. The cadet had been operating a tractor in a field. After the rescue he suffered burns to his hands and back. When he left the palace after receiving his award, WO Buckee recently recovered from plastic surgery, was by chance, standing in the crowd by the palace gate when he caught sight of the Cadets 'Scawfell' Flash; he re-introduced himself. Both were later interviewed by the BBC.

Many more crashes occurred, a Miles Master at St. Bees, a Vickers Wellington and crew never recovered from the sea off St, Bees Head a Hawker Audax near Mirehouse Pond, a Grumman Avenger above the Screes at Wasdale, along with a Hawker Hurricane at Black How Cleator.
Millom and Cark were the RAF training aerodromes. The number of flights, with young inexperienced crew members, included many accidents throughout the region, (approximately 34 spread over the four establishments).

Whitehaven Borough Council, under the Mayor Alderman Harvey, also did their bit. After setting up an **Emergency Committee** to Co-ordinate War Work, a **Municipal Piggery** was formed in buildings rented from the Lowther Estates for £25 per year, at the Rope walk. It started in 1940 with 30 pigs as a nuclear stock for breeding and fattening, and by 1941 had sold 71 pigs at a very handsome profit.

Mayors Church Service 1940

A Typical Anderson Shelter.

Air Raid Shelters

The first public ones were opened on the seventh of December 1940. When it was realised that over 50 people (the threshold) were employed at the Town Hall, an air raid shelter had to be provided - so a cellar was converted at a cost of £45, with 7 shillings in the pound being claimed back from the Government.

The public had access to shelters in the cellars of Somerset House, Duke St and 14 Scotch St (which had room for 175 persons, converted at a cost of £475. 12/5d), also in

A Morrison Shelter.

OLD CELLARS BECOME AIR RAID SHELTERS

Whitehaven is Well Prepared

WORK is rapidly being completed on the conversion of 10 large cellars in Whitehaven as air raid shelters.

These will accommodate about seven per cent. of the total population. They are not intended for regular use, but are provided for the safety of those who may be caught on the streets or in the cinemas at the time of an air raid.

The entrances are fitted with thick baffle walls to prevent casualties which might be caused by bomb splinters, and, while they can be effectively sealed against gas, those who use them are expected to carry their respirators with them.

No shelters are to be built on the outskirts of the town. In cases of emergency people will be directed to the cellars by air raid wardens who will be on duty.

Old cellars become air raid shelters

A Deep Shelter under the Savings Bank

the cellar of Montague Burton's, under the Co-op grocery on Duke St, Shipping House West Strand, under Spencers Brewery Queen St, Knowles & Fiddlers Preston St and the Savings Bank on Lowther St. These 'deep shelters' held a total of 1900 people and each had a small blue light over the door as a guide. However, there were 23 surface shelters some at White Park and Bransty school, but there were problems at **Monkwray School**. The children's first shelter was in the old brickwork's tunnel, a good shelter. There was two problems-it was a long way off, and they had to cross the 'brake' railway!

Salvage Week-Cutting the Railings from St Nicholas church.

If householders were in a situation where there was no garden in which to put an **Anderson shelter**, then they could apply for a free **Morrison shelter**. This was made from steel and was to be used indoors, (it also doubled as a large table).
If your income was over £350 per annum then it was going to cost you £7. One was placed on show in the window of the Corporations Electricity Company's showroom, on Lowther St.
There were very few installed, and the complete apathy found in the Ennerdale Rural District, caused many memo's and meetings of the Civil Defence Committee for months to come.

The **Medical Officer of Health** reported that 25 Children and 15 expectant mothers had attended the artificial sunlight clinic. Also that the Infectious Diseases notified were, Pneumonia-2, Whooping Cough-2, Scarlet Fever-1, Dipheria-1, and Tuberculosis-1. He had also set up an **expedient mortuary** on Preston St. with Mr Thomas William Lucas, as Superintendent to be paid £4 10s/week and a female assistant at 5s per case; a local photographer was also to be on call. A War Dept dentist was also on hand at 23 Lowther St.

Local Children were supplied with free National Dried Milk, fruit juices and cod liver oil. Among the many restrictions placed on them, was that no kites or balloons had to be flown, or they were deemed to be contravening the Prohibition Order 1941. (Balloons & Kites).
They collected scrap metal, newspapers, old rags and woollens. In the season they collected rose hips, and took them to school where they were paid 2/- a stone.

Dig For Victory Campaign

The Council backed the national campaign. Land was rented for allotments and St. Bees golf course was dug up and cultivated. A competition for the best kept allotment was organised with 1st prize of £3, and a separate competition for Elementary school children.
There were eventually 600 members, who paid a shilling fee. This entitled them to seed potatoes, lime and fertilizer, at half price, as well as films and lectures.
It was said that the most influential gardener this century was **Adolph Hitler**, as every garden was now full of Anderson Shelters or vegetables - three million tons were produced (nationally) in six years, even commercial nurseries were only allowed 10% of their output to be flowers.
Technical support for gardeners was readily available from the radio, with regular articles in the daily press, along with some films that were shown at special venues.

Salvage Week - A Dump on Duke St.

The putting green on **Flatt Walks** was changing. It had a Giant 10,000 gallon emergency water supply (EWS) tank placed on it, the other was placed at the Duke St. End of Castle Park.

A Prefabricated Nursery for 40 children was also sited there. It was opened on the 7th December 1942 with Nurse Banks as the Matron, at £200 per annum and Mrs Platt as her Deputy.

The charges were 1/- (5p) per/day for one child inclusive of meals (provided by the Schools Canteen Service), to be paid 1 week in advance, however it was closed on Sundays.

Fire Service.

The fire station was in Scotch St. It went through the same changes as most local stations, ie supplementing of regular staff by the Auxiliary Fire Service **(AFS)**, then taken over by the National Fire Service **(NFS)**, in early 1941.

March the sixth 1940 was the fire brigade's red 'engine' day. Whitehaven and Ennerdale's new fire engine-the 'last word' in fire fighting, was delivered - a powerful six cylinder 80hp Leyland, with a two stage turbo pump, delivering 5/ 700 gallons per min.

Fully streamlined, with a Francis 11 searchlight, and seating four, it cost £1,545. Later in the day it was taken for pumping tests at the dockside.

The engine was in use at a major fire on 18th January 1941. This time it was at St Bees School. The entire south wing of foundation house was gutted. This contained the studies' block, OTC centre, and its armoury. No one was injured, but this was the third time in the life of the school that the same wing had suffered from fire.

The Grand Hotel

Another large fire on 21st January 1940, at the Grand Hotel, when one woman from Workington (Miss Taylor) was killed, and Whitehaven's premier hotel, was burnt to the ground. The AFS under Chief Officer, W Crone attended the sad scene. With six inches of snow on the ground the water from the hoses turning to ice. Workington AFS arrived to help after 25 minutes after experiencing a hazardous journey on bad

The Grand Hotel after the Fire.

roads. They were too late to save the young girl who died after being overcome by smoke, and was found later still in her bed, which had crashed through two floors. Lieutenant W. Devine and Sergeant Jack Cartmell helped in the fire fighting duties. Fireman Aaron Housby and Captain Charters of Workington, were injured. The Hotel guests were given drinks and clothing by the landlord of the nearby Shipwright's Arms.

Then in Febuary '41 one of the oldest and best known Inns," T'Wooden Steps" (Punch Bowl) was on fire. One of the two sisters who had been inside had been trapped, only getting out by jumping 14 feet from her bedroom to the ground. The 'Jumper' was young Betty Johnston, who was leading a charmed life, as she had escaped from the Grand Hotel fire a year previously, but suffered a sprained ankle this time.

November 1944 and another drama, the Chief Officer of the Town Brigade Mr H O'Neil was sacked after 37 years service. This was too much for the volunteers of the NFS- so a protest meeting was held in the 'Vine' and thirty five turned up to give their old Chief Support and encouragement.

After he had been presented with a wallet from Engineer Welch, in a short address he thanked them, and said that if his expertise could be of any help to the brigade, he would 'willingly assist' but was never asked.

Captain. H. O'Neil. NFS

Wartime Appeals

Whitehaven's Member of Parliament.
Mr Frank Anderson said that in 1940 he had attended 907 interviews, and on 83 visits, he had spent a total of 101 days in the division.

In a speech to the Whitehaven Traders Association held at the Central school on March 10th 1939, he said, *"We need the incoming industry from European refugees and Industrialists, also better rail and road links. But in more than one case, West Cumberland has been chosen because of the fine character of the working people in the district, by those Industrialists who have settled here recently. My final words to you are; Don't turn back; Go ahead; have confidence, by that, I am sure, victory will be yours"*(loud applause). The Mayor then said that Whitehaven's MP was 'tireless in bringing trade revival to the special areas, and we could ill afford to lose his stewardship to the front bench.'

Mr Frank Anderson MP.

The **Whitehaven News** like most other papers, was constrained not only on the news they could publish, but also had difficulties obtaining the raw materials to make its editions.

The reporting staff had volunteered for active service (of the eight who went, only four survived, and of the four remaining, two were wounded). The paper acted as a focal point for the various **wartime appeals** which were promoted by the government and funded by buying bonds or savings certificates.

1. Warship Week

The papers appeal for warship week brought in more money from the Whitehaven, Ennerdale and Millom rural districts than the target of £75,000. In total £197,000 was collected by Whitehaven borough for **HMS Whitehaven**, and £115,000 by Ennerdale and Millom for a Corvette **HMS Loosestrife**.

HMS. Whitehaven, was a "Bangor" class minesweeper built at Dartmouth by Messrs, Philip and Son. She was launched on the 29th May 1941, and completed on 14th November the same year.

She arrived on station at Alexandria, to carry out duties with the 14th Minesweeping Flotilla, Mediterranean Fleet on 6th June 1942. She was able to sweep for both magnetic and accoustic mines and displayed Whitehaven's coat of arms on her quarter deck. It had a long career for a warship, and a busy one. During the invasion of Sicily she broke the boom into the harbour and landed explosives experts to clear the port. She

HMS Whitehaven

was then attacked by shore batteries and aircraft but escaped. Not only was the ship adopted, but the crew also. Many comforts and letters were sent to them from local people to the ships home ports.

Before being scrapped in 1948, she was awarded Battle Honours for the Atlantic, Sicilian and Normandy, campaigns.

St James School Pupils who raised £1 12s for the Spitfire.

Whitehaven & Ennerdale's Spitfire

2. Spitfire Week

Run from September 23rd to the 29th 1940, targets were set for towns and villages, and again the target of £5,000 was easily reached, the surplus was sent to the RAF Benevolent Fund.

A cheque for the Spitfire was handed over and a Spitfire 11B, P8588 purchased, proudly bearing the name **'Scawfell.'** Built by Vickers Armstrong at their Castle Bromwich Factory, it was delivered to service on the 26th May 1941, and saw service with **610, 616, 315 (Polish) and 132 Squadrons**, being damaged during a forced landing at RAF Peterhead and scrapped in November 1941, It had lasted four months, a short span, during its busy and active life, during the Battle of Britain.

The methods used to raise money for Government Appeals seemed to be rather varied, but generally included baby shows, boxing tournaments (boys), whist drive, film shows and the ever popular dance.

3. War Weapons week

Raised £142,610. The Boroughs target had been £70,000 (with Ennerdale Rural district) from March 29th-April 5th 1941.

To mark this achievement, one of the largest parades took place on a Sunday, reviewed by the Mayor, Dignitaries and Col Burns-Lindow. The parade was a mile long, led by the Border Regiment band, followed by small units of the Navy, Border Regiment, Pioneer Corps, RAF, Home Guard Units and WAAFS, then members of the British Legion (Bransty & Hensingham).

Next came the Whitehaven Borough Band followed by contingents of ARP, Civil Defence, First Aiders, Nurses, Voluntary Aid Detachments, Fire Brigade, Rocket

Brigade, Guides, Scouts, ATC, and the Boys Brigade.
And as an added touch, Fighters and Bombers flew over the parade, performing aerobatics to the crowd's delight, the whole day being rounded off by a public meeting in the Gaiety Cinema.

Capt. LS Maitland-kirwan RN, Taking the Salute.

4. Wings for Victory Week
Held during the week of May the 8th to 15th, 1943. The government required £160,000 for the funding of two Lancaster Bombers, from Whitehaven Borough, the grand total £202,000 being achieved. Ennerdale Rural Districts target was £100,000, for two Lancaster's and two Spitfires, £163,000 was raised by buying savings' bonds or certificates.

5. Tanks for Attack Appeal
The appeal needed £66,000 from Whitehaven and Ennerdale district to buy two tanks for our armoured Corps, so it ran from 3rd August to 12th of September 1942.

Royal Visit
Whitehaven had a **Royal Visit** by Prince George the Duke of Kent, on the 3rd of July 1941. He arrived dressed in his RAF Group Commanders uniform. He inspected Naval, Military, and Civil Defence Units, Members of the Home Guard, Fire Brigade, Auxiliary Fire Service, Nursing Auxiliaries and the Woman's Volunteer Service. Later in the council chamber, accompanied by the Mayor (Ald JB Smith) he talked with the twelve widows and mothers who had been bereaved in the William Pit Explosion.
Those presented were Mrs Burney, Mrs Harker, Mrs George and Mrs McGrievy who all had lost their sons, then Mrs J. Wells, Mrs W. Perry, Mrs J Curwen, Mrs C

Ald J B Smith Mayor.

The Duke inspects ARP Personnel.

Moore, Mrs R. Baxter, Mrs J O'Pray, Mrs C Martin and Mrs S Barbour all miners widows.

The rest of the afternoon was taken up with a descent into Haig pit accompanied by Sir Harry Haig, Mr FA Carr (High Sheriff), Lieut. JA Lowther RNVR (his private secretary), Mr J Williamson (general manager, Whitehaven pits), Mr A Gardener (manager of Haig pit) and Messrs T. Brannon and W. Thompson, miner delegates.

HRH The Duke of Kent, ready to descend Haig Pit

Tea was taken then HRH spent the night at Muncaster, visiting Barrow the next day. Sadly HRH (an experienced pilot) was killed on active service, along with the Hon John Lowther, on the 25th August 1942, flying as a passenger in a Sunderland flying-boat that crashed in the North of Scotland, en route to Iceland.

The Drill Hall

Situated between Catherine St and Flatt Walks, it was the home of the 309 Field Reg. TA. After the Territorials had done extensive training in this country, they were then sent into combat. The drill hall then became a training establishment for local TA recruits, under the watchful eyes of Sergeant Majors Belch and Usher, and Captain RE Christopher, 5th Battalion TA. Battery. Sergeant Major Dan Vigar MBE was the long serving storekeeper, in the hall, up to 1945.

Evacuation

West Cumberland was classed as a safety zone, so when the ARPs were presented with Gas certificates, in the Gaiety cinema in 1939, the Mayor gave the figures of a recent accommodation survey. There was, he said, 22,950 habitable rooms in the borough. So on the formula of one person per room 5,208 more people could be accommodated, however it was decided that only 4,7337 places would be sufficient.

Egremont Councillors with Young Evacuees 1940.

That was the plan, reality was to prove different!
The ratios were to be -Unaccompanied children; 1,712-teachers and helpers; 505-children accompanied by parents/guardians; 1,197, accommodation arranged privately with relations etc.; 753, to help this influx 1,137 more mattresses were needed along with 2,274 blankets.

So on Friday the 1st of September 1939, over 750 children arrived at Egremont in two special trains from the Northeast, with a further 300, at Millom. They arrived with gas masks and labels bearing their names and home addresses, many with mothers, some with teachers. People offering homes (Billets) were paid 10s. 6d, for a single child and a further 8's 6d for an extra child or mother.

Evacuees and their Teacher at Egremont.

These allowances may have looked generous however 1941 prices were approx., 2lb loaf of bread 4d, pint of milk 4d, butter was 1's 7d per lb., cheese 1's 1d per lb.
Whitehaven's evacuees arrived at Bransty Station the same day. The first was the entire school of 500, from Heaton boys Secondary School, who made a lasting impression on the town when they marched four abreast to the Central school to be allotted their billets.
In total 10,000 evacuees came into the districts during the first week, and 10,200 in the second week,
At St Bees the Staff and pupils of the famous Mill Hill school, shared the public school, also the Seacote Hotel as Staff Common Rooms.
Throughout the war years the number of evacuees 'ebbed and flowed' throughout the region, first it was the Tynesiders, then people from Barrow, followed later by Londoners escaping the Blitz.

The Home Front

Muncaster Castle

This was the scene of the strangest evacuation, when on 24th of August 1939, millions of pounds worth of art treasures left London in three special LMS Railway containers. These included well over 800, oil and water colours, from the Tate Gallery, plus treasures from India House. The local villagers who helped to unload the crates, had no idea that they were handling Constable's *'Valley Farm,'* Millita's *'Christ in His Parent's House,'* the *'Blue Boy'*, and the famous *'La Baignade'* by Seurai. The largest was Copley's *'Death of Major Pierson,'* the smallest at 12 inch's, Coteman's *'Drop Gate.'*

Nine men from the Gallery stayed in the castle, and guarded the chambers with their treasure, day and night for over six years, cooking washing and cleaning for themselves. However at Christmas their families, were allowed to visit, the dinner being provided by Lady Ramsden.

Whilst it may have been a lonely -boring vigil, it was better than being in London, for the Tate Gallery was extensively damaged by bombing. Returning the crated paintings after hostilities, went smoothly except for the very large paintings.
British Road Services were asked to deliver them, but the local depot only had flat lorries in its fleet, so the work was contracted to a young Mr Robin Coates from Howgate, Whitehaven. Robin and his Commer cattle wagon travelled to London accompanied by two armed guards. After unloading he was given a bed for the night, in a large central heated room, inside the Tate Gallery. The journey took two days but he was back in time for his regular runs - to Cockermouth and Whitehaven auctions. He never carried a more valuable load, for the largest crate measuring, 8 by 12 foot, carried Copleys *'Death of Major Pearson'* its value today - a cool £1.4 Million.

Mining

Most of the pits were operated by the Coltness Iron Co, the parent company of the Cumberland Coal Company (Whitehaven) Ltd. Managing Director Mr DJ Barr, Mr A Crowe Chief mining engineer, Mr J. Williamson General manager.
The local pits in production included Haig, William, Harrington Nos. 6,10 and 11, Walkmill, and Moorside Drift,

A 47 year old miner was directed to work at the Lowca (Harrington No 10) pit. When he did not turn up for work, he later told the **Tribunal,** that the last bus would have gone to his home, at Cleator Moor, before his shift was finished, leaving him stranded.

'Bevan' Boys.

The Chairman told him that 3/6d could be claimed, to find overnight accommodation, *"Will have I to live away from home?"* the miner asked, the chairman's reply was "Yes, fined £10 for not complying, next case."

The reason the authorities were getting tough, was that 80,000 of the youngest miners in the Nation's deep pits had left to enrol in the armed forces, or the munitions industry. In Cumberland over 1,000 had left. The average age in some deep pits was now 41.

The mining industry was now subject to the Essential Work Order (EWO), and (a white paper in '42) the industry was supposed to be under state control, but the Minister of Fuel and Power of the day, said We have 'too little influence on the day-to-day management of the pits', and that Managers were 'trying to serve two masters,' the companies and the state.

The manpower situation was serious; so in 1943 when youngsters came of age for National Service one in ten was picked out by ballot to work in the pits. To some youngsters from middle-class, or professional parents this was a profound shock, and some say that it did more to highlight the miner's lot, than anything before or since.

Some refused to work in the deep pits and were jailed -40% appealed (most lost). In the end only 21,000 'ballottees' entered along with 16,000 optants.

Vital coal production had continued to fall, 204 million tons in 1942, 194 million in '43, 184 million in '44, and 175 million in '45.

Cumberland's target for 1942 was 29,400 tons at the pit head, and 25,000 tons of saleable coal, after the extraction of dirt. There was a 6% increase at Haig, and 14% at William Pit (bonus to be paid). However, the Cumberland coal field as a whole, was working 9% under par.

A desperate national attempt in open cast mining using large imported American machines, in 1944, only resulted in an extra 8.5 million tons. Meanwhile, the pits became increasing dangerous, lack of good timber, steel and rubber, and many small seams being worked, added to the danger; well over 5,000 miners died during wartime. Accident figures released showed that there was 1 serious accident (off for 3 days or more) per four employees.

Local miners were no strangers to danger. On the third of June 1941 an explosion rocked the **William Pit,** The cause was spontaneous combustion of some pillars of coal in old workings. The explosion that followed, burst through into other bands and the main 'highway.' The Manger and Deputy were already down the pit, so they turned back to help, but the disaster had already claimed 12 lives, and injured 10. Fire was raging in part of the pit, so after the bodies had been recovered, the burning part was sealed off for ever. In later years this pit would earn notoriety as the most hazardous in Britain.

Conscientious Objectors

The treatment of objectors was more humane than in WW1, mainly due to the Conscription Act 1939. Gone was the public shaming, and women no longer gave white feathers to young men on the street. Provision had also been made for objection to military service, on political, as well as pacifist grounds.

All had to appear before local tribunals who gave exemption to genuine cases or directed others to 'suitable' work.

In the first call up national statistics showed that 22 in every 1,000 objected, and the total figures '39/'45 were 59,192, over four times the number in WW1.

Only 3,577 were given unconditional exemption. Nearly half (28,000) were registered as objectors only on condition that they took up approved work, generally in agriculture, or stayed in their work. Over 14,691 registered for non combatant duties in the armed forces and 12,204 were turned down, and remained liable for National Service. Approximately 1,400 went to jail, including 400 women.

C. Os, were tolerated by the public during the 'phoney' war, but they turned against them in 1940, (after Dunkirk). Some were sacked by employers and 120 local authorities dismissed them from service.

As a result of the 'National Service (Armed forces) Act, the Cumberland & Westmorland Conscientious Objectors Tribunal was formed at Carlisle, with His Honour Judge Peel OBE. presiding, assisted by Mr CR Boothby and Mr A Stephenson, (National Union of General and Municipal Workers). An indication of the hearings were:-

• One 20 year old joiner said he was 'sick all the time.' The judge said he would let the doctor decide.

• A 21 year old pipe fitter-who was also a preacher and averse to the taking of human life. He was registered for non-combatant duties.

• The 22 year old bricklayer from Maryport was rather more outspoken. He said *"it takes twenty years to make a youth, yet a stray bullet can kill him in a second"* and *"there is only one King and everything belongs to him."* - Registered by the tribunal as an objector.

• A Keswick joiner (23) said he was not prepared to do military service, but would help the down and out. He was told to join the St Johns Ambulance Service.

• The coke ovens driver (22) was told to remain in his job, as it was contributing to the war effort.

However, being registered did not mean that they were free from criticism. It was alleged that a C.O had taken a job vacated by a combat volunteer at Clifton Colliery, and a strike was only averted by the management paying him off. It is said that he left 'defiant.'

Aliens

Mario Gulani (60) a Swiss confectioner who had lived in the town since 1910, was found to be on Inkerman Terrace, away from his house during an air raid, this was in violation of the Aliens Act as it was after 10:30pm. During his court appearance it transpired that if bombs had been falling on the town he would have broken the law, even by going into the shelters to avoid danger.

Many aliens were interred on the Isle of Man, and some tried to escape. On the 18th of October 1941, three Dutch fascists arrived on Eskmeals beach, having stolen a ten-ton yacht from the Island, complete with engine and sails. They were GJ Schop (32) a pilot, DN Van de Boon (28) and J. Merman both ships' officers. The plan was to make for the 'Irish Free State 'and then make their way home to Holland. Something went wrong, and the vessels engine failed.

Then in storm conditions the yacht was tossed up and down the Solway for days. First they were sighted off Barrow then up to Annan, then back off St Bees Head, finally grounding on the shore at Eskmeals, where PC Maylor and the military had been watching and waiting with some amusement. When they found that two ships' officers were on board, their smiles at the apparent lack of seamanship grew even larger.

After being transported to Whitehaven, they were taken to the public wash house, then given dry clothes. Next day, after being identified by the IOM police and photographed, they were taken back and jailed for 6 months.

Youth Organisations

Whitehaven **Air Training Corps**. - Scawfell Squadron, (Whitehaven & Ennerdale). Part of the Cumberland and Westmorland Wing, No 1030 Squadron. The President was Major General Sir John Ponsonby CMG, DSO. with Chairman WH Wandless, Secretary H Williams, the Commanding Officer Flt Lt AT Bennet.

At the initial recruitment over 100 boys, aged 14 to 18 joined, their studies included physical training, mathematics, signalling, motor engineering, wireless telephony, radio construction and drill.

An appeal went out for instructors and equipment ie. old radios, Morse keys, and earphones. Again the people rallied round and donated equipment to the boys, who by now, wore their new, smart blue uniforms.

Smart they looked when they paraded outside cinemas, to draw attention to the new RAF film 'Target for Tonight'. A Ministry of Information film that won an Academy award.

Time was spent at Millom aerodrome helping to service aircraft, and attending lectures, given by front line pilots. Their enthusiasm abounded when they were given their first flight, in twos and threes depending on the type of aircraft. On one trip, the plane came down on a temporary airfield rather hard, slightly injuring one cadet, who arrived back at camp in the early hours of the morning, woke every one up, showing them his bruised chin, and bandaged finger. His talk of a possible medal proved to be the last straw!

The first Cadet to gain his RAF wings was H. Raymond Dodd of Foxhouses Road, he joined the RAF in 1942 and became a Halifax Bomber Pilot, carrying out 40 missions and gaining the DFC.

Women's Junior Air Corps.

The girls formed the **Women's Junior Air Corps,** 300 turned up at the inaugural meeting and after a comprehensive address by Miss Walker - the Area Commandant for the WJAC, Mrs J. Craw was elected Unit Commander, Chairman Miss J. Cowie, Secretary Mrs AG Henderson, Treasurer Miss E. Wallace.

The Officers were, Mrs M. Atkinson, Miss I Clark, Miss D. Kitchen and Miss P. Murray. This formed part of more than 200 branches, which had been set up after the King made an appeal for more youth organisations.

Girls could pick activities from;

PT	Games	Swimming
Drill	Boating	Camping
Land/ Air study	Study of clouds	Theory of Flight
Study of Aeroplanes	Engine theory	Morse code
Use of Electric /Gas	Wireless	

The Corps uniform consisted of a blue Glengarry cap and blouse, grey skirt, black shoes and stockings. There was no money for these items, so the girls had to buy them, and surrender precious clothing coupons. There was also a fee of 3d per week for subs. Initial funds were obtained from the proceeds of a dance, held in the Empress Ballroom.

Sea Cadets

One of the first in Cumberland, (formed in 1942) with over 50 members. They paraded and drilled in the Irish St school, and were given free uniform and equipment. Activities included seamanship, signalling and dancing - "the hornpipe".
They were presented with a ship's lifeboat to practice seamanship on, by a wealthy local man Mr John C. Kennaugh, who was now a partner in a Liverpool firm of Marine engineers.
Later the War Department gave them a building on the harbourside, which had

Sea Cadets at Practice

recently been vacated by the Royal Marines. This eventually became the Training Ship 'Bee' named after the small vessel that had left Whitehaven to fight the Spanish Armada.

Guides

On the 12th of June '43 the Chief Guide - Lady Baden-Powell visited, accompanied by the District Commissioner Miss E. Wallace. The local guides were drawn up in a 'horseshoe' on the Whitehaven Secondary School field to hear an address entitled

Lady Baden-Powell Chief Guide (Near Flag).

Lord Somers Dept Chief Scout, Inspecting Cubs at Kells.

'You are the future.'
Juvenile Delinquency
There was a problem with **juvenile delinquency**, so the Home Office bought Ponsonby Hall the once stately home of the Stanley Family.

It was renamed Pelham House School, (an 'approved' establishment) for boys between 12 and 15 years old. These were generally the wayward sons of fathers who were in the forces, and from homes all over the North. The average time spent in the

Pelham House Athletic Team 1941.

school was somewhere between 18 months and 3 years. Mr Hewetson was headmaster to 70 boys, who followed a rigid but competitive regime. They were also taught manual trades.

Occasionally local youths would 'kick over the traces' and one 17year old from Egremont who was sent to farm work at Ulverston, did so in spectacular fashion.

He ran away from the farm but crept back in the night, slept in the barn and then stole provisions and a rifle.

Walking over fields he reached Askam. Then after loading his hoard into a stolen boat, he rowed out into the Solway. All this exertion made him tired, so he fell asleep for many hours, losing an oar in the process, which he discovered on awakening.

Provisions were consumed and after three days he was rescued off the Isle-of-Man, (under nourished and rather green in colour) by a steamer who dropped him off at Ayr in Scotland.

After being transported back he appeared at Barrow court where he was bound over and had to pay 35/- costs for the theft of 1 rifle, 1 oar, 4 tins of beans, and 2 tins of cocoa.

Entertainment

Entertainment was also of the War Time variety. Courses on War-Time cookery were held in the Electricity Showrooms on Thursday evenings-and Kells Community

Cinema Adverts

Mr BD Wood International Chess Player at Whitehaven.

Centre showed its first colour Film, 'A Garden Goes to War' made by Plant Protection Ltd.

The Area had many Cinemas, The EMPIRE, GAIETY, QUEENS, KELLS, CASTLE -Egremont, PALACE - Frizington, ENTERPRISE - Distington

In addition, there were BBC Broadcasts from local factories, including two "Workers Playtimes" from the High Duty Alloys Canteen, and featuring the Distington Band.

One was overheard by a Whitehaven soldier, Sapper Richard Coyles of the 79th Armoured Brigade, as he scanned the radio frequencies of his Sherman Tank, in Normandy. It was of particular interest to him, as he was originally a Border Regiment musician, and his uncle Peter Coyles was in the Distington Band.

Mr W Logan with the Champion Puppy 'Lightship'

Wartime Industry

Edgard's Staff Machining Demob Suits.

H. Edgard & Sons, London
This family firm evacuated from London and was originally staffed by Hungarian and Czech refugees. They occupied the old fibre mill at first, but then moved into a purpose built Factory at Preston St. They turned out 2 million uniforms, battle dress, RAF clothing, leather jerkins and fur-lined outfits for ATS gun crews and some special waterproof uniform for tank crews which were so complicated that they were made up of 145 parts of material. Some of the key workers were victims of the London Blitz, and were only too pleased to be in Whitehaven. The factory had over 400 employees - mostly women. Welfare included music while you work, canteens, savings group, and a social organisation.

L. Silbertson & Sons Ltd
This firm had made its name as one of the few, who were experts at cutting the Bearskin Headress for the Brigade of Guards.
Based at Cleator Mill, with a workforce of 500, they made uniforms for the three services. They designed and produced uniforms for the Burma Campaign. Later, they manufactured uniforms for London Transport and the GPO.

Smith Brothers
The four hundred and twenty employees, manufactured cellulose film that was made into small bags, used for the wrapping of biscuits in emergency ration packs. These were used by all the services.

Girls from the Silk Mills.

West Cumberland Silk Mills

Another West Cumberland Industrial development Co. initiative. The factory took over 17,000 sq. ft. of Raikes field at Hensingham, and when in full production, it made over one million miles of nylon, producing 120,000 parachutes for the war effort. Later they made ties for 'Demob' Suits.

Hensingham Silk Mills Staff

Kangol Co.
Set up in 1938 at Cleator Mills, by Jacque Spreiregen to produce the Basque Beret. Production then switched to berets for the armed forces, initially there was a workforce of 64, mainly girls.

Marchon
In 1941 Fred Marzillier and Frank Schon made firelighters from wood and chemicals in Whitehaven. Late they moved to Kells, where they manufactured chemicals, mainly detergents. Later Frank Schon was knighted. The factory employed over three thousand workers.

Eugene Ltd.
Employed 260 in their two factories at Whitehaven and Cleator Moor, producing cosmetic packs, for the women's forces.

Royal Ordnance Factory Sellafield 1943

Royal Ordnance

Although they were outside of Whitehaven, the two giant Royal Ordnance Factories, had an effect on the town as they needed provisions, raw materials, transport and staff.

In 1939 plans were made to build the two TNT factories. Both had to be in a safe area with plenty of water, and a steady supply of workers. The first completed was **ROF Drigg** in 194. It covered 341 acres and contained its own railway system.

Next came **ROF Sellafield** started in 1942, and built by John Laing and Co. of Carlisle, who employed 3,419 contractors to build the complex, which reputedly cost £3, million. It began production in May 1943. The site contained nitrate buildings (Reveted), boiler houses and laboratory blocks (later bought by Marchon) and 82 process buildings. These were inter-connected, along with 26 admin buildings. This site also had its own 30 inch narrow gauge railway system.

Workers were brought to work by the railway but this could not cope with the shift systems, so the Cumberland Motor service buses with their grey double-deckers with wooden slatted seats were used. Many of the workers were housed in hostels at Millom, Silecroft, Stanley Gill, and Beckfoot Eskdale. The scientists were housed separately at Irton Hall.

The munitions and raw materials were brought in by the railway without mishap, but on 22nd March 1945, a munitions train with 10 tons of depth charges on board caught fire. The train's fireman Norman Stubbs from

Fireman HN Stubbs GM

Aftermath of Explosion Nr Bootle Station

90

Harrington, bravely uncoupled the burning wagons, but they exploded.
The blast left a crater 45 foot deep, and 100 foot long, sadly the driver died in the accident. Norman was later awarded the George Medal for bravery from the King.

At Eskdale 37 people were employed by Vickers Armstrong, and Beckfoot Quarry with its extremely hard rock walls was used to test top secret explosives for D-Day.

VE Day

German radio announced the unconditional surrender about lunch time on May the 7th. This caught the people of Whitehaven by surprise. But when they heard the official announcement that the next day was to be 'Victory over Europe Day' and a holiday, the town came alive.

Bunting, and flags appeared on houses, and vessels in the Harbour were bedecked with signal flags which including 'Plague and No Water.' There was a bonfire in Castle park that illuminated the hospital, where a giant red, white and blue 'V' sign

Winner of Egremont Ploughing Competition Mr T Southward

was lit up on the roof. The dancing in the park and a star shell and rocket display, lasted until after midnight.

The next day a united service was held in St Nicholas Church. The Rev CE Nurse officiated, and the Mayor's chaplain Rev JA James in his address said *"There was a feeling of relief and thanksgiving, after defeating the new pagan's of a well ordered military power that had threatened the Christian Civilisation."*

Church Bells rang, dancing at the Empress and Oddfellows Ballrooms followed. Cinemas were full.

The Borough of Whitehaven held a belated celebration day on Monday, June the fourth Castle park was again put to use, with children singing in the morning, and a band concert and dance that finally finished at 11:30pm. There was also an Invitation

Winter 1940, Wath Brow Mission Church.

dance at three p.m., in the Enterprise Ball room, for returned prisoners of war, and service men / women on leave.

At **Egremont** factory girls paraded arm-in-arm, singing "Its all right Mademoiselle". There were dances in the streets, buntings appeared, and among the flags displayed was one that was a antique, for it had Lord Robert's head on it; the Boer war had been over for forty four Years!

The homecoming party for Pte. Joe Weir (POW) was to be held in the Market Hall, but the party developed, and most of Egremont danced at Joe's party, which lasted long into the night.

The festivities continued for the next two days with dances, socials and children's parties, plus a free matinee at the Castle Cinema.

Distington

Distington junction station

This typical West Cumberland village may be taken as a replica, of others in the area, the same essential wartime organisations existed in them all.

Distington has been called 'one long street'. That it may be, but in 1939 the by-pass had already been open for two years and the village was a hive of activity, even though over one hundred, of its inhabitants were away in the forces.

Coal was still being mined at Walkmill, Harrington No 10 and Dean Moor. The north of the village was dominated by the large alloy factory, High Duty Alloys (HDA), where work was carried on for twenty-four hours, seven days a week, employing 3,000 people.

The whole factory was camouflaged and surrounded by light anti aircraft guns (LAA). The home guard unit that helped to protect it, ('E' company 5th Border) was based in the old Lilly Hall farm buildings.

Next to the factory was the busy station and junction of the Cleator and Workington Junction Railway.

By the railway station, was a small prisoner of war camp. This held men who worked on local farms. One farmer bought a bike for his prisoner-labourer and corresponded with him for years when he was repatriated back to Germany. To provide themselves with pocket money they would make or carve small artefacts or toys, to be sold locally.

The camp was the centre of a manhunt in 1945. An 'ardent Nazi' went missing, he was found next day lying in St Joseph's RC Church at Workington, with cut wrists. He recovered later and was sent to a more secure camp.

The village seemed to attract strange aircraft, and already mentioned was the giant HP 42E that force landed near West Croft farm Pica, then in 1942 a Supermarine

Walrus amphibian crash landed in a field alongside the Gilgarran road, fortunately without injuries to the Naval Pilot. PC Lowther guarded it until the military took over, it was later dismantled and taken away by road.

Another Industry in the village was based on the garage premises of Myers and Bowman Ltd. The large buildings were used to manufacture a small tipping trailer for the ministry of Agriculture. So robust were these that spares were provided up to the 70's. Local ladies were employed in the manufacture. Another part of the works was used to refurbish vehicles for the Ministry of Defence.

Home Guard

A unit, part of the 6th Battalion was formed in Pica (45 men in the HG & 36 in the Forces) and Distington, the latter had two Officers 2nd Lt Joe Rudd and Lt Raymond Scattergood, Jack Roberts from Common End, was the sergeant. The unit's quartermaster stores were in the Enterprise Ball Room. Parades and drill practice took place behind the Hope & Anchor Hotel, or if wet, inside the ball room.
Rifle practice took place at the at the long quarries on Barfs, and a check point was set up in the small arches of the 'Dragonfly' railway bridge.

The National fire service (NFS) had its pump and equipment store on Main St. On Sunday mornings the pump was towed by Myers & Bowmans bus to the beck at Mr Briggs farm, where the NFS held their practice. This unit was called out to a large fire that was burning at Pattinson's mill in Whitehaven.
They arrived so late that the fire was out, but the leader apologised. One of his men had held them up, he could not get his wellingtons on because of his corns.

The ARP had been formed by the Rector Charles Joseph Warren. The warden's post was situated at 56 Main Street. Tragically the Chief Warden was killed on duty. He and another warden were in the Black Cock area, checking on lights allegedly showing at Bellevue, when they were hit by a car. The Chief never recovered. And it is fitting that his name is included on the local war memorial.
Wardens were JD Crone, David McLean, John Messenger, JW Mitchell, J. Mossop, Alexander Hamill, Thomas Graham, Alfred Crone and Walter Tinnion.

The School was closed on the first of September 1939. This was to give the authorities time to billet sixty-two evacuees

Rev Charles Joseph Warren

from Newcastle, in the area. The school re-opened four days later with the evacuees attending the school along with three of their teachers.

In the coming years the children carried out air-raid practices, gas-mask drills, distributed knitted garments to the forces and raised over £5,000 by the sale of Bonds/Certificates for War time funds.

Great enthusiasm was shown for the salvage drive to collect scrap metal, rubber, paper, rags and bones. These skills helped when the government stopped them heating the school with coal before the first of November. So the children simply collected wood, lit the fires, and then settled down to their lessons.

They were rewarded with two days holiday for VE day, and two more for VJ day, when the Infants won 30/- as a prize, for the best decorated lorry, in the Distington VJ celebrations.

It must have been exhaustive living in the village in 1941, because of all the activities and social events, but there was a purpose; most of the money raised went to war related funds.

Activities over two weeks, in 1941 included:

Distington Council Meeting, *held in the reading room, the agenda was:*

- *The letting of Toll Bar allotments.*
- *The Globe Hotel allotments.*
- *Proposed gas supply to the village.*
- *News that the Common End telephone box, was paid for.*

Distington Church Council. *Held a whist drive, which was won by Mrs P. Freeman, Miss Penrice, Mrs Tinnion and Mrs Douglas.*

Distington Homing Society. *Where the results of the young birds race from Kings Norton were 1st and 2nd H. Allen, 3rd J. Kennet and 4th G. Wilkinson.*

Distington Unemployed Centre. *Another whist drive where Mrs Douglas and Miss Penrice won again.*

Distington Labour Party. *Held a dance in the Enterprise Ballroom, music by Billy Iley's Jazz Jesters from Maryport. Stewards were Mr A Rowe and Mr J. Murray. The refreshments were provided by Mesdames E. Dixon, W. Hays, J. Stabler, S. Gorry.*
Organisers were Mrs D. Beattie and Miss Atkinson, and £18 was raised for the fighting services fund.

Distington British Legion. *Held a meeting of the Darts league in the Black Lion. Official's present were J. Mitchell, Chairman, F. Watt, Secretary and J. Casson, Treasurer.*

Victoria Hall. *A dance in aid of the fighting services fund was organised by Mr & Mrs Dorney, to Don Kelly and his Tango Band. Stewards were G. Bayliff and S. Leighton.*

Mothers Union. *Had an Aid to Russia collection, and raised £4, 6s 9d at their meeting.*

Distington ATC *(Scawfell Squadron) paraded in the Ball Room, under Flt Lt W. Wilson.*

Dyon School. *Raised £600 to buy bren guns for the war effort.*

Rehearsals by the Male Voice Choir, and Dramatic Society, *and a practice by the Distington Broadcast Orchestra.*

Distington's VE Day celebrations were rather contentious. The villagers thought that the Distington Parish Council was taking too long, to have an official celebration, so they went ahead collected funds and organised their own children's day. This was too much for the DPC and a row broke out, because, said the DPC the collections were 'unofficial' but at last a compromise was reached.
Heavy rain spoiled the day, but there were prizes for the best dressed house, and one for business premises.
Miss Doreen Hodgson was crowned the Victory Queen, 600 children sat down for tea in the Enterprise Ballroom, and 200 pensioners had their tea in the Victoria Hall. In the evening there was dancing in the Enterprise, to the Paramount Orchestra from Clifton. The next day was given to sports, aided by Fletcher's Amusements

Bibliography.

Attack Warning Red, *the History of the ROC-*   ISBN0356 084116

Most Secret War- *R V Jones* -   ISBN 0 340 24169 1

The History of the 5th Battalion Home Guard *(Border Reg.)*.
 Major E G Sarsfield-Hall. KMG.

Wartime Women-*Dorothy Sheridan*   ISBN 0 7493 0741 2.

Front Line County-*Andrew Rootes*   ISBN 0 7090 3473 3.

The Last Ditch-*David Lampe*   ISBN 0 30492519 5.

No Time to Wave Goodbye-*Ben Wicks*   ISBN 0 312 03407 5

Conchie-*Ernest Spring*   ISBN 0 85052 189 0